Theatre Across Borders

OTHER TITLES IN THE THEATRE MAKERS SERIES:

Notes from the Rehearsal Room: A Director's Process
by Nancy Meckler

Toward a Future Theatre: Conversations during a Pandemic
by Caridad Svich

The Uncapturable: The Fleeting Art of Theatre by Rubén Szuchmacher and translated by William Gregory

Adrian Lester and Lolita Chakrabarti: A Working Diary
by Adrian Lester and Lolita Chakrabarti

Movement Directors in Contemporary Theatre: Conversations on Craft by Ayse Tashkiran

Contemporary Women Stage Directors: Conversations on Craft
by Paulette Marty

Julie Hesmondhalgh: A Working Diary by Julie Hesmondhalgh

Julius Caesar and Me: Exploring Shakespeare's African Play
by Peterson Joseph

The Actor and His Body by Litz Pisk and introduction
by Ayse Tashkiran

Steppenwolf Theatre Company of Chicago: In Their Own Words
by John Mayer

Theatre Across Borders

Abhishek Majumdar

methuen | drama
LONDON • NEW YORK • OXFORD • NEW DELHI • SYDNEY

METHUEN DRAMA
Bloomsbury Publishing Plc
50 Bedford Square, London, WC1B 3DP, UK
1385 Broadway, New York, NY 10018, USA
29 Earlsfort Terrace, Dublin 2, Ireland

BLOOMSBURY, METHUEN DRAMA and the Methuen Drama logo are trademarks of Bloomsbury Publishing Plc

First published in Great Britain 2023

Copyright © Abhishek Majumdar, 2023

Abhishek Majumdar has asserted his right under the Copyright, Designs and Patents Act, 1988, to be identified as author of this work.

For legal purposes the Acknowledgements on p. ix constitute an extension of this copyright page.

Photograph © Pallavi MD

All rights reserved. No part of this publication may be reproduced or transmitted in any form or by any means, electronic or mechanical, including photocopying, recording, or any information storage or retrieval system, without prior permission in writing from the publishers.

Bloomsbury Publishing Plc does not have any control over, or responsibility for, any third-party websites referred to or in this book. All internet addresses given in this book were correct at the time of going to press. The author and publisher regret any inconvenience caused if addresses have changed or sites have ceased to exist, but can accept no responsibility for any such changes.

A catalogue record for this book is available from the British Library.

Library of Congress Cataloging-in-Publication Data.

Names: Majumdar, Abhishek, author.
Title: Theatre across borders / Abhishek Majumdar.
Description: London; New York: Methuen Drama, 2023. | Series: Theatre makers | Includes bibliographical references and index.
Identifiers: LCCN 2022043237 (print) | LCCN 2022043238 (ebook) | ISBN 9781350195288 (paperback) | ISBN 9781350195295 (hardback) | ISBN 9781350195271 (adobe pdf) | ISBN 9781350195264 (epub)
Subjects: LCSH: Theater and globalization. | Theater--Philosophy. | Intercultural communication in the performing arts. | LCGFT: Essays.
Classification: LCC PN2041.G56 M35 2023 (print) | LCC PN2041.G56 (ebook) | DDC 792.01--dc23/eng/20221116
LC record available at https://lccn.loc.gov/2022043237
LC ebook record available at https://lccn.loc.gov/2022043238

ISBN: HB: 978-1-3501-9529-5
PB: 978-1-3501-9528-8
ePDF: 978-1-3501-9527-1
eBook: 978-1-3501-9526-4

Series: Theatre Makers

Typeset by Deanta Global Publishing Services, Chennai, India
Printed and bound in Great Britain

To find out more about our authors and books visit www.bloomsbury.com and sign up for our newsletters.

In memory of
Dipali Majumdar and Elyse Dodgson

For Rai,
Hoping you grow up in a world with less borders and more art

The writing of this book was supported by New York University
Abu Dhabi, Arts and Humanities Division

CONTENTS

Acknowledgements ix

Introduction: Travels and questions 1

Part I Home 19

1 The quest for tradition 21

2 Language of theatre 36

3 The enterprise 49

Part II Away 61

4 Brecht in Kashmir 63

5 The Kashmir trilogy 77

6 The writing of *Pah-la:* A theatre journey across the roof of the world 95

7 Devising in the Tibetan Transit School 127

8 Reading George C. Wolfe's *The Coloured Museum* in a New York subway 141

9 Hamidur Rehman: A journey through Bangladesh and Germany. A journey about a journey 154

Part III Other Geographies 171

10 Lessons in pausing: From a theatre in West Africa to a monastery in the Himalayas 173

11 On censorship 185

12 The pandemic and the theatre 198

Bibliography 213

ACKNOWLEDGEMENTS

Several people have made this journey possible. Too many to be named and thanked in the space of a page. So, I first begin with an apology for not being able to thank everyone. My gratitude is not bound by this page.

Thank you,

To begin with, Anshuman Acharya and Jocelyn Clarke, who have been my friends and dramaturgs throughout this journey.

Chris Campbell at Oberon books for commissioning the first version of this work.

James Hogan and Charles Glanville at Oberon for believing in me throughout the years and publishing my work in English and Hindi.

Anna Brewer for being the brilliant editor she is and for imagining this book with me.

To my teachers and students around the world.

To Pallavi Krishna for being with me through large parts of my theatre-making life. To have seen and experienced its many ups and downs with me. For making the journey to Tibet. I will always be grateful.

To the Shikhar family for being mine too.

To Susmit Sen, Anmol Vellani, Arundhati Ghosh, Sarita Vellani, Arundhati Nag and Mahesh Dattani for their support over the years.

To Madhilika Sen for her belief.

To MD Pallavi for being a close collaborator and friend of recent years and for reading the chapters and commenting on them. It has been invaluable.

To the Royal Court Theatre for being my theatre home away from home. To Vicky, Lucy, Richard and Sam.

To Tibetans and Kashmiris who risked immensely to tell their stories.

To Anne Cattaneo at the Lincoln Centre.

To Bangalore Theatre community.

To Ranga Shankara, Bangalore, for being my theatre home. For being my place of solace and refuge. For being the default theatre in my head when I make work.

To everyone at Indian Ensemble and Nalanda Arts Studio.

To fellow artists who have been part of this journey. To the translators in many languages who have translated my work and directors who have staged it. To artists who have breathed life into my images and words.

To Irawati Karnik and Sandeep Shikhar for being the reason I can sign up work in so many places in the world, knowing you are always there. For your friendship.

To my sister Joyeeta for opening this world of stories for me and putting up with me as I wandered through childhood. For being my rock.

To New York University Abu Dhabi for supporting this work with a research grant and for being my home in the world. To Bob Vorlicky for helping me understand the shape of the world.

To the Inlaks Foundation and Richard Alford of the Charles Wallace Foundation.

To Riad Mahmood Education and Arts Foundation for supporting my early work. To Head Start Educational Academy for supporting me in my early years.

Most importantly, to my daughter Rai. This book and all plays are made on stolen time from you. They are yours.

Introduction

Travels and questions

I

This book is an ode to the diversity of theatre-making in the world. It is an enquiry into what makes for this diversity and an examination of the variety of motivations that people harbour in different parts of the world to make their theatre.

I have been fortunate that I found the theatre and the theatre accepted me. Most people in this world never find out what is the thing they can do while doing which they can forget the future and the past – the task that makes them completely focus on the present. This, I believe, is what we mean by 'calling'.

Unfortunately, the barriers to the discovery of one's calling can be so many in an astoundingly unequal world that most people may not discover this at all. Even when they do, many a times their socio-economic realities might be so unsurmountable that they might not be able to pursue that calling. Even if one is able to follow that calling, for many people, the particular calling they believe is theirs may not accept them with ease. May not accept them at all.

This is not to say that one must think of these possibilities while pursuing what one believes is their 'calling', but only to say that I have been very privileged.

The theatre has given me a lot in my life. It has given me the ability to be present in the moment with complete attention as long as I am in the theatre space. It has given me joy, exhilaration, love, relationships and friends. It has given me my home, my suitcase, my work and my sense of the world. The theatre also very importantly has given me a place to ask questions, something I had in plenty always. The theatre has also allowed me to travel enormously, again something I had always wanted to do.

In fact, the theatre has always been about travel and questions for me. These are the two most important aspects that brought me to it and kept me in it. As much as this book is an attempt to share with readers around the world whatever little I have learnt or inferred from these years of travel and theatre-making, it is also a book of gratitude to theatre-makers around the world.

It is about acknowledging that there are infinite ways of making theatre and infinite reasons for making theatre, which sometimes get lost in the larger narrative of those theatres in the world that have either a large market or enormous government subsidy. This can sometimes give a false impression that the theatres in London's West End or New York's Broadway or the state-sponsored German houses have automatically by virtue of their scale achieved some deep universal insight into form and content.

The title 'Theatre Across Borders' is in one sense practical and in another sense, romantic.

Practical because there *are* borders. Physically, our world is divided into very specific borders of nation state and other more deep-rooted borders of religion, caste, gender, sexuality and race that are often forcibly imposed on people. These borders allow certain people to travel to some places and not to others. This translates to extremely disparate ways in which we can access each other's cultures. The barriers may not only be in terms of visas. It may also be deeply socio-economic.

Many practitioners in the Global South may never have access to each other's works to begin with. Ironically, it is much more viable to receive a grant or fellowship and travel to the Global North than to travel to another place in the South.

The Global North on the other hand is deeply impoverished because many practitioners do not even realize that they can actually travel to other places and learn from them. The pressures of the theatre industry in the West are so high that just to survive in the theatre industry of New York or London might occupy someone's entire lifetime.

But the title is also romantic because one wishes that the more abstract boundaries, once pointed out in the chapters that follow, will help us get 'across'.

It is ironical that although theatre is a site of questioning, this site itself in many contexts can be deeply parochial. There are so many in-built ideas in theatre of what is 'good', 'experimental', 'national', 'modern' or 'traditional' that theatre programming and education are often completely trapped in these concepts without questioning them. Everywhere in the world, one can find elaborate discussions about why that theatre is theatre and the other theatre is either something completely different or an experiment. The overemphasis on being cutting edge and new, on being original, authentic or being five-thousand-years old is, in my humble opinion, a huge barrier to what is fundamentally of value in the theatre.

And what is of value in the theatre is what is in front of us. In any context, it rests on what is being asked, who is being entertained, and very importantly, how are time and space being treated in front of us.

World over, from Tibetan Buddhist monastic performances in the Himalayas to street-theatre in North India to open-air theatre in north Africa to the giant state-funded theatre of Berlin and Hamburg to the well-known playhouses of London and New York, these are the only four consistent factors at play in my view. And these factors can never have a formulaic approach. No culture can decide for the other the way this should be done. No culture has, so to speak, 'cracked' how to do it. The world is not automatically aligned to this osmosis, but some effort in this direction can be hopefully enriching for everyone.

This book, in a way, is an invitation. To travel. To ask questions. Together.

It is an invitation to break these walls as much as possible by making theatre in different places and contexts. With people we don't know, in front of audiences who are not known, and so, find connections between our lives using this extraordinary art form.

It is also an invitation to think about where one is. To think about the criticality of one's specific town, lane, community, local market and specific political and metaphysical questions. For without this, theatre can easily become tourism. And at the same time, to think of this 'local' in relation to the world. This attempt at discovering a local in a global context is the romantic reason for the 'across' in *Theatre Across Borders*.

In these years of theatre-making around the world in different contexts, I have learnt that we are different. That multiculturalism does not mean to make everything one. In fact, it is to be able to recognize, celebrate and learn from the differences, thereby making all these different locals richer. Otherwise, we are left pursuing an imaginary global that looks more like a duty-free shop where there is everything and yet nothing of anyone's in particular.

Theatre Across Borders is an attempt to share some ideas of the theatre I learnt from home, some that I learnt while being away from home (and that could be learnt only if one left) and some which are from no place in particular. Hence, this book is divided into its three parts of 'Home', 'Away' and 'Other Geographies'.

II

Travel

When I was a child, my world was quite small territorially. I grew up in Delhi in the 1980 to 1990s, in the campus of Jawaharlal Nehru University (JNU), where both my parents worked.

JNU is located within the old Aravalli hills that reach this part of Delhi from Rajasthan, a desert state in western India. It has a beautiful one-hundred-acre campus that was, at that time, largely a forest. Our house was in the staff quarters, and my travels were mostly inside the campus. My father used to take me on his bicycle around the campus, which in those days was full of animals. There were parts of the campus that had deer, parts that had bears and other parts which had wild pigs and peacocks. One of my earliest memories is of travelling in this university campus on my father's bicycle, the two of us having an adventure pretending we were on a treasure hunt of some sort. And the treasure was often something quite simple, a fruit most of the times, but the hunt made it seem like the biggest thing in the world.

I also walked with my mother to another part of the campus, where she used to run a primary school for the children of non-professorial staff. I used to love being in her class. The classes were taught in Hindi and the school was essentially two large rooms and an open space. This was a very different world and a different travel compared to where I travelled with my father. This was in the part of the campus that had been established many years ago and was called Old campus.

In many ways, Old campus was reminiscent of socialist buildings around the world, much like the structures in East Berlin. It had large buildings, the university's bank and post office, and a co-operative market to buy essentials. On either side of the road lay two different worlds. One, a city more organized than the organic shape that the city of Delhi had taken. And the other, a complete forest.

This was the beginning of travel for me. Holding my mother's hand and the handle of my father's bicycle sitting on a tiny seat in the front.

However, I also travelled a lot inside the campus with my sister. She is eight years older to me and I went wherever she went. For the longest time in my life, I had no plans of my own, no ambition, no real decisions about where to go or what to do, and the sole purpose of my life was to just tail her as much as possible. I would often accompany my parents when they went to drop her to her school bus, and from the time she came back, I just followed her everywhere. Even to her friends' houses, playing around where she played, much to her annoyance – I am sure – at that age.

And of course, I had my own friends. Many of them with whom I played on campus. But there were large sections where we were not allowed to travel on our own for fear of wild animals and snakes. So, there were boundaries to where we could go on our own.

Within this travel, there were several moments to watch performances. The legendary Indian theatre director Habib Tanvir would sometimes come with his theatre company, Naya Theatre ('new theatre' in English), and rehearse in JNU. There would be a great buzz all around, and every evening, the whole campus would gather around his open-air rehearsal to watch his company rehearse. After that, many of the actors would be invited to people's houses for dinner.

We also travelled to see Ram Lila, to attend music performances of classical music late at night and film screenings during Durga Pujo, a festival about which I have written in a chapter to follow.

Performance and travel were thus intricately linked for me inside the campus. There were no cars, no scooters that I remember of. We walked or went on bicycles. There were two buses in the campus which were so infrequent that my primary memory of these buses is to wait for them.

A few years ago, I went back to the campus with my wife and daughter, and was shocked to realize how small everything was. The playground was really tiny and the houses were small as well. I realized I remembered them as being large because I was a small boy then.

It is this illusion of size that might have also given me these early memories and fascination for travelling and theatre. Most of the places I am referring to are now accessible within a few minutes by car, but when we were children, it took a long time. The journey was part of the experience and I think travelling and theatre have this in common. Both are experiences and not ends. And both use time not in an absolute but in a relative sense. Our memory of theatre and travel is deeply connected to who we were then.

Hence, travelling became an intrinsic part of my association with the theatre, and perhaps, this is why my own theatre life later on has been so intrinsically linked to going to different places. In a way, I am perhaps subconsciously still seeking the comfort of my father's bicycle and my mother's hand through the theatre.

While travelling through different theatre landscapes, I also feel that most people make theatre to relive something. To find something that is deeply within them but in the real world there is no way of reliving it. Hence, while from outside our worlds, theatre buildings, dramaturgy might be all very different, deep inside there is this common desire to recreate a feeling, a moment of great love or trauma and experience. Only, this time with some distance and control, so that it can last as long as we want to and then we can carry on with our present lives.

In a way, the entire act of theatre-making is a way of travelling. To another reality. Only to reveal what we really are deep inside.

III

Questions

JNU is also a university campus notoriously known for its spirit of questioning. When I was growing up, the place was abuzz all the time with students and teachers sitting in different corners of the campus engaged in heated and animated discussions on various subjects.

The campus has always been extremely diverse with students from both urban and rural backgrounds. Their diverse realities informed their academic interpretations, and these interpretations led to a culture of questioning on campus.

In my own house, every evening, there were gatherings and discussions. I had nothing to do with them because I was playing most of the time. However, this was the backdrop of my childhood: this sense of questioning that percolated into us.

When my father took me for these bicycle rides he would invariably ask me several questions about what I had seen and made of the forest. My mother read to me and also introduced me to the world of music. She spoke very little but a lot of her interaction with my sister and me were in questions. When we saw a play or a film, heard a new album or read a book, she would often ask us at the dining table about it – not only what we thought of it but also very importantly asked us to give reasons for our opinions.

However, I think the person who encouraged me the most to question was my sister. I would perpetually be a student in her mock class. She would pretend to be a teacher, put up a small blackboard and take classes of subjects ranging from molecular biology to *Mayor of Casterbridge*! She also asked a lot of questions and in these questions were the prompts for me to learn.

My mother was religious. My sister prays and has a small temple in her house. I was never religious and no religion was imposed on me. If I asked something about a myth, my sister would tell me what it was but I was never asked to believe in anything that they did.

My father's elder brother lived with us for a few years. He was an old man who in the afternoons would read the *Ramayana* and *Mahabharata* aloud. I used to detest his attempts at making me listen to these stories, but I understand now what a deep impact it had on me to listen to him every day. Most importantly, he too read the stories for me like long tales, and although he was a devout believer, he never asked me to believe in them with religiosity. He wanted me to know the epics but not necessarily revere anything.

As I grew up, my entire academic life became a series of different kinds of questions that I pursued. From mathematical to developmental to artistic to metaphysical.

In a way, whatever is there in this book also stems from questions about the world. And I can easily say that the greatest gift my home gave me was a spirit of questioning. Perhaps this is also why I took to the theatre and moved away from pursuing exclusively the other subjects that I was pursuing in my academic life. Theatre gave me the breadth to explore different kinds of questions. It gave me the opportunity to ask questions endlessly, never imposing on myself to make up my mind.

In time I realized that at the heart of every great play lies a question. These questions are sometimes realized effectively and sometimes, not so much. However, without these questions, a play loses its significance in its own time, let alone in history.

It is these questions that keep the play alive through the years because although contexts and particulars change, questions seem to be significantly eternal in our society.

Through time immemorial, literature itself has played this important role. To question the powers. When it comes to the theatre, this gets even more compounded because not only is one reading the text but the text is being played out live, which makes the questioning more palpable, real and dangerous.

In the Indian classical tradition, there is an interesting origin story about the theatre. The story (very briefly) goes like this:

At the end of a hundred-year war between the gods and the demons, the gods finally came back to heaven and met Vishnu (the preserver god). Vishnu asked the gods to describe how the war unfolded and as the gods tried to recreate the events.

Seeing this, the demons thought that the gods were about to attack again. Flustered by the disrespect towards the ceasefire, they pulled out their weapons and prepared for another round of battle. The gods stopped and told them: 'We are not really attacking you, we are telling Vishnu what had happened.'

This led to the demons becoming suspicious of the gods. They asked the gods, how would anyone know if they were really attacking or merely retelling the story with actions.

The gods went to Brahma (the creator god) and asked him what could be done about this problem. Brahma very quickly understood that the story of a hundred-year war with its many complexities, ups and downs, would need to be told in a new form that would need to combine many different skills. Hence, he took Words, Movement and Music from three different Vedas and passed it on to a sage called Bharata, who had a hundred sons. Bharata then taught and trained his one hundred sons both in the form that had just been created and on the particulars of the story. The sons diligently rehearsed until show day in heaven.

The gods sat eagerly, announcements were made, Vishnu and Brahma sat at the helm and the much-awaited performance began.

Initially, the gods were terribly excited on seeing themselves being represented in this manner. They started to relive the moments of bravery, exhilaration, fear, laughter and doubt. However, soon something else started to happen.

The gods realized that the one hundred sons of Bharata were performing the story from the perspective of the demons, and in fact, what they were doing was that they were questioning the gods. The gods got very unhappy since they were not only the producers of the show but also the producers of the form!

Miffed, they went back to Brahma to ask him about what must be done. Brahma concluded that since this form was being practised by the common people, with a mix of forms and aesthetics, it would always ask the gods some difficult questions. Hence, Bharata and his one hundred sons were banished back to earth, where they would have the licence to spread the form and practise it as a tool to continue the questioning of the gods.

I find this story fascinating for a variety of reasons.

First, it tells us that the storytellers had to practically learn the form in order to tell the story. I think in modern theatre, this is truer than ever. Theatre is perhaps one of the very few forms world over wherein a practitioner must always create a form for a project. The moment we get the form for a play, we cannot ever use it again in the same way.

Second, we tell the story from the perspective of the vanquished and ask difficult questions to the powerful and not the weak.

And third, if the play succeeds, often the players are banished. Even today.

There are specifically three questions that have interested me immensely in my life. When I look back at my varied interests since childhood, I find these questions repeating in them. A lot of my own theatre work revolves around these three questions although I have realized this only while writing this book. It has not at all been a self-conscious endeavour over these years to engage with these questions. It has just so happened to be.

I also think every theatre culture and theatre-maker has some questions that they keep returning to. And if we have to understand or learn from another theatre-maker or culture, it helps to know these questions. They tell us what drives individuals and communities to make theatre. It also helps us understand how to collaborate with other cultures if we engage with these questions.

The chapters in this book stem from the questions that have driven my journey. These may not be the same for others at all. But I do believe reading this book might be a different experience when the reading is coloured by my questions. However, in no way is it a must to engage with them. I encourage the reader of this book to keep or discard my questions, depending on whether it is aiding or hindering their reading. The important thing is to read through the prism of their own questions. If they overlap, it might be a pleasant coincidence. And if not, I am even more grateful to the reader for engaging with the material with their own separate questions.

The first question that has often driven me is, 'What is the invisible?'

Since childhood, I have been fascinated by that that cannot be seen. One of my cousins was a magician of some repute. He used to travel with cards in his bicycle because people would often ask him to show magic tricks wherever he went. I used to love being with him, and all the magic tricks which involved invisibility fascinated me. History as a subject fascinated me because it was making so many invisible things visible to us in the classroom. Eventually, mathematics and chemistry interested me enormously for the same reason. I was fascinated by the world of molecules and atoms and used to wonder that so much was going on with things I could not see.

In theatre too, I loved this the most. The bits when something completely invisible would suddenly manifest. I loved the ghosts, the djinns, the fairies, the witches in the stories I was told and the plays I saw.

At a certain stage of my life, I gave up engineering to study pure mathematics also for this reason. I enjoyed the beauty in abstract algebra much more than I enjoyed knowing about machines. Not that I have not had to learn about tools and techniques later. Theatre is a lot of engineering often and one has to learn about material and mechanics, but this did not come naturally to me. When I decided to finally pursue theatre, the love for the invisible was definitely something that drove me to make the decision. And world over, I think a lot of theatre is about making the invisible visible. If we are to understand and appreciate a different theatre culture, we must engage with its invisible. That is where its impulse lies.

The second question that has always intrigued me is, 'What is a society?'

I think this triggered in me consciously sometime in my university days. I was briefly studying rural development, and one our professors took us to the remotest of villages to make us understand first-hand the realities of rural life as most of us were from the cities. My own interest in rural development came again from the first question. It was an invisible world to me. I knew that India was largely rural and that, by and large, the access I had in the world was an exception. The literature I enjoyed during my college days was full of references to village life. And at some time, I was also deeply interested in doing something in economics, which would be a better and more real use of my skills in mathematics than putting it in service of some large corporate.

In one such village we were visiting as a class, we were offered some lemon juice. We were in the side of the village where the Dalits lived, the so-called lower castes in Hindu society. (The caste system divides Hindu society into four strata: the untouchables, the lower-caste workers, the warriors and the priestly class. The caste system is illegal and yet in India it is the most distinct marker of identity.) We were sitting and having a discussion there when it came up that the voting office was in the upper-caste side of the village. The man who was telling us about the upper-caste side would not turn to see the village polling office but point his finger towards it while looking at us. After a while, when someone asked him about it, he told us that they were not allowed to *look* at the upper-caste side of the village, let alone go there. Not even look.

On the way back, I asked my professor then how does that Dalit man vote. He told me this is what you should be asking and this is why boys like you who grow up in Delhi need to step out to know what the world really is. Sitting in Delhi, it is very easy to have a picture of the world and make all the laws of the country with those assumptions.

After some time, we interviewed another person of the same village. A young man who worked in a nearby big city as an autorickshaw driver. This man was upper caste and shared a room in the city with a Dalit boy of the same village. However, the moment they arrived by bus to their district bus station, they went separate ways. In the city, they were known as people from this village who spoke in their dialect of Oriya (a language of eastern India). But when they reached closer home, their caste identity became paramount.

This raised important questions that have stayed with me since: What exactly is a society? How do we call ourselves a civilization? And in a world of fluid identities, how does power play between the same people depending on which identity they choose to, or are compelled to, perform at that time?

The great Indian writer U. R. Ananthamurthy said that identity in India is fluid. He said that we say we are Indian only when we are not in the country. When we are in India, we say we are from this state or the other, which are divided by language. When in Bangalore (in his case) or in any such big city, when someone asks us our identity, we say the name of our village or district. And he beautifully said that these are not 'competing' but 'continuous' identities, and that people in general have no problem in identifying themselves as participants of these continuous identities. However, the moment we are manipulated to make these identities competing, there is violence, distrust and discrimination.

I think this is true for the entire world and not only for India. Every human being is participating in continuous identities and not competing ones. Society is a slice of this continuum. Which is why we exist in multiple societies in the same day.

However, in our workplace, in our national politics and based on our religious or gender identities, sometimes we are given the simplistic framework of competing identities, thereby creating the 'clash of civilizations' theory, which is hugely flawed in my view.

In a way, a lot of my theatre life is about examining our continuous identities, and hence, this book is also arranged in order of this continuum. Its parts start with 'Home', move to 'Away' and then to 'Other Geographies' because for me, and for most theatre practitioners, the theatre can be very liberating as it makes us aware of our existence in this continuum. It is our job to protect the theatre from narrow frameworks that restrict our identities to one industry or tradition.

The third question that has intrigued me is, 'Which patterns are beautiful?'

I have always been fascinated by patterns – on walls, in glass panes, in car number plates, in colour on clothes, in leaves, on tiles on the floor, in mathematics and music; I am a pattern addict. I love observing patterns since childhood. While driving, I continuously multiply car numbers and find intriguing patterns every day. I read random timetables of train services to seek out patterns. One of my most favourite pastimes is classical music (Hindustani and Carnatic largely but also some Western music) because of their incredible ability to evoke emotion through patterns.

Theatre-making is also essentially, like any other temporal art form, a play of patterns. When we introduce something in a play, the essential exercise is to discover when it becomes important and when it exits the story or stage. Different cultures and theatre traditions have found different answers to the problem of what is the most suitable pattern to tell a story that is meaningful to its community.

My love for patterns is also one of the main reasons why I am in the theatre, as it allows me to delve in patterns and structures of words, movement, objects and ideas eternally. A lot of the technical elaborations in this book are really elaborations of pattern. In a way, I am elaborating on the way patterns work in theatre-making and the diversity of these patterns. It is again an invitation into this beautiful world of patterns in order to appreciate theatre from different cultures. In my view, it is extremely important to recognize that good dramaturgy is essentially a meaningful pattern in the backdrop of assumptions within a culture. Otherwise, there is a risk that in the name of internationalism and being clear to an audience, we end up reducing all beautiful patterns to the same formula by applying too strictly the narrow appreciation of one system.

With this backdrop, the parts and even the chapters that follow can be read in any order. I believe the chapters stand on their own, and one can directly read any of them without needing to read the previous chapters leading to it. However, within the 'Away' section, it might be helpful to read the chapters on Kashmir and Tibet in their given order.

The book starts with the section 'Home' because that is where my journey started. Many people say they have many homes. I think this is partly true for me too. I can be at home in many places. I am at home in London, in parts of New York, in Delhi, Bangalore, Calcutta, in mountains in North India, but essentially home for me is very clear. Home for me is in India and someplace where there is a river and a tree. I am completely at rest there. I can live in many places but I know that deep inside me there is a movement towards a tree which is next to a river.

However, my work is not necessarily *about* home. I do not think that an artist is less effective when they are away. Since time immemorial, what we know about India is through travellers. The earliest accounts of India are through the journals of the Chinese traveller Fa-hien in the fifth century AD and Al-Biruni's *Tarikh-ul Hind* in the eleventh century. I very strongly believe that what we know about our home can be hugely informed by our travels. The world is set in a context. We understand our context better if we can travel.

However, in the part of 'Home' are the roots of everything I have learnt. My view of the world I imagine is mediated through this. If my continuous identities did not include being Bengali, being from Delhi, an Indian with English, Hindi, Urdu and Bengali, I would not have been the person who I am. The privilege of being a man, and in the context of India, someone who was born in an upper-caste household, has undoubtedly given me a lot of privileges compared to others in my country. Hence, my own theatre practice has been a close examination of the limitations and privileges of these continuous identities.

Hence, the book starts with 'Home'.

'Home' has three chapters.

The first chapter, 'The quest for tradition', looks at a young artist's search for tradition in the early years. Many young artists universally go through a phase where they have a real need to know what do they belong to. What is it that will hold them as they sail their creative boats into the choppy waters of uncertainty? And this quest for who I am and what is my theatre is akin to asking where do I come from. For a theatre-maker, the answer to 'Where do I come from?' can hold the key to many ways in which they can approach and understand their creative life. However, unless someone is born and raised in a singular form that is specific to a region where one continues to live, the question of tradition becomes extremely complex. Especially for people like me, who grew up in an urban landscape in a country like India where there are in fact many traditions at play.

This quest at one stage of my life felt vital. And even now as I teach and work with younger colleagues, I find this deep desire to know what is one's tradition. This chapter elaborates my own quest for tradition and where I think we need to look for the answers to this question.

The second chapter is 'Language of theatre'. This is about the many languages of theatre that we speak in around the world and an attempt at unpacking what we fundamentally create when we say we are creating theatre. Hence, when we say we are curating or watching international work, or work from another context in general, how do we genuinely recognize the particularities of that language of theatre rather than observing or, worse, creating cosmetic differences?

In today's times, when several theatre practitioners like me move across geographies and contexts to make work, it becomes all the more important in my view to be able to recognize that within the theatre, we are continuously changing languages depending on the context and location of the work. This chapter is a case for celebrating these many languages and an invitation to recognize what lies underneath.

The last chapter in this section is 'The enterprise'. It looks at the relationship between theatre ecologies and the art itself. I teach in a university where we have students from more than eighty countries. In several years, I would have in a class no two students from the same country. This also means that all of them come from completely different theatre ecologies and what it takes for them to make theatre back home involves extremely diverse sets of actions.

World over, young theatre-makers often wonder how to get started. What do they need to make good theatre? Do they need an industry, a social revolution, a historical imperative, funding bodies or drama schools? One of the key things I learnt from home is the importance of recognizing the theatre ecology one is in and shaping one's theatre enterprise accordingly. This, to me, was a vital lesson because I find that in many parts of the world, young people can feel really bogged down thinking they do not have the market or government support one has in New York, London or Berlin.

Chapter 3 looks at the companies I grew up around and the companies I formed with others in India, and it also examines the different systems I have had the opportunity to work in.

The second section of the book is 'Away'.

It begins with two chapters on Kashmir. Culturally, one could argue that Kashmir is very close to my context. However, politically,

I am completely convinced that India is an occupying force in Kashmir. There is a territorial dispute in Kashmir only because India and Pakistan have tried to compromise its autonomy. Hence, I have kept my chapters on Kashmir in the 'Away' section. Politically, I would cringe at calling Kashmir home due to the nature of our relationship with the place, but this is again a place where I am definitely *at* home.

The second of these chapters, 'The Kashmir trilogy', is very important in my life. Even when I was in drama school in London, I was sure for some unknown reason that I will come back and work on telling stories from Kashmir. What shape it would take, I did not know. But I knew that this would be important to me. The trilogy of plays I subsequently wrote on Kashmir taught me immensely about collaborating, about development of form and the politics of content.

The next two chapters, 'The writing of *Pah-la*: A theatre journey across the roof of the world' and 'Devising in the Tibetan Transit School', are a peek into the making of *Pah-la*, my play on the Tibetan struggle and the future of non-violence. The work on *Pah-la* has been one of the greatest experiences of my life as it made me think deeply about non-violence, freedom and the connection between dramaturgy and cultural context. It also presented to me the enormous power that culture has in the world and why political forces invariably want to control the narratives and cultures of those they are occupying. *Pah-la* also brought to me the richness of Tibetan art. As a playwright and theatre director, it taught me enormously about the power of theatre in the world.

The chapter on the Tibetan Transit School is also a look at the craft of acting itself. This comes from a workshop I did with Tibetans who had escaped from China and walked across the Himalayas to reach India. It examines what they brought to the floor as actors and also looks into the 'training versus experience' debate that is often present in the art of performing.

'Reading George C. Wolfe's *The Coloured Museum* in a New York subway' is a chapter on race and on reading plays with the city as a backdrop. It is about a way of reading that actually centres the society that the play is meant to be in dialogue with. On my first visit to the United States for the Lincoln Centre Directors Lab, I was struggling to find my place in New York City until I started to read this play in the subway in and out of Brooklyn. This play took me to Black churches, neighbourhoods, schools and rehearsal rooms, and opened an enquiry into how we can bridge the gap between where the theatres are located in a city and where the people are whose stories need to be told in the theatre.

The next chapter, 'Hamidur Rahman: A journey through Bangladesh and Germany. A journey about a journey', is about the making of a play on the life of Hamidur Rahman, a Bangladeshi asylum seeker in Germany who eventually committed suicide after attempting to cross Greenland on foot. This chapter is about intercultural collaboration, its challenges, joys and learnings.

The last part of the book, 'Other Geographies', delves into three significant experiences in my own journey and, I believe, in the journey of many theatre-makers in subtle or overt ways.

'Lessons in pausing: From a theatre in West Africa to a monastery in the Himalayas' looks at the importance of silence in dramaturgy and how our understanding of pauses in different dramatic traditions and contexts can enrich our understanding of dramaturgies around the world.

'On censorship' is a look into the different kinds of censorship that theatre-makers face even today. Two of my own plays have faced severe censorship: one in India and the other in China. The writing of these plays led to threats, coercions and attempts to buy out the plays.

Censorship can operate in different ways and I believe that theatre-makers of the future need to be very alert as to when they are being censored. Because unlike earlier times, nowadays, censorship can be very effective in guise. Art institutions and governments often have to walk the line of wanting to appear liberal, albeit within socially accepted norms. It is in this context that this chapter attempts to unpack the many modes of censorship that we are inadvertently working under.

Finally, 'The pandemic and the theatre' looks at the enormously different ways in which theatre around the world adjusted to the pandemic. The challenges that arose from it and, particularly in the context of the Global South, what the pandemic really meant for theatre-makers and audiences.

These twelve chapters are by no means an exhaustive academic study of theatre. They are a snapshot of the journey of an artist who has had the privilege of creating work across cultures. They are a conversation. An argument and an invitation to question.

Part I

Home

1
The quest for tradition

I

My first play as a writer and director was an adaptation of a Bengali novella. I had read the book in English, but it was immediately clear to me that this is something that I would like to make in Bangla. Eventually we made two productions. One in Bangla and another in English.

While writing it, I never faced any writer's block. While directing it, I cannot think of any major nerve-wracking problems either. There was a sense of great freedom while I was making it. We had a largely Bengali cast that overlapped between the two productions with some exceptions. The play opened at the Ranga Shankara theatre-auditorium in Bangalore.

I still remember, clearly, the first blue light that came on stage with the music. That image has never left me and it never will. It was the most extraordinary moment of self-realization. A moment in which I came to know what I really wanted to do and should be doing with my life. I thought this was something that came naturally to me and that the theatre and I were made for each other.

However, this notion did not last long. From my second play onwards, everything seemed like a struggle. I tried to make work using everything that I was learning in the many workshops I had been attending and through all the work I was doing as an actor. For a few years since then, I tried to use all my tools to tell a story well, but even if the plays worked well, it was never as effortless as the first time. Initially, I attributed it to beginner's luck but although I believe in destiny to some extent, I am not a believer in the smallness of luck. What had happened was that I was failing to find an inner image of the plays that I was making. Something that I was able to find quite seamlessly in my first play. It felt like I had lost an essential gift. I had neither the craft as yet to pull off my early flamboyant staging ideas nor did I have the internal image of the work which would guide me when the craft failed.

I went to London on a scholarship to study at the London International School of Performing Arts (LISPA), which taught a Lecoq-based theatre course. We had students from all over the world, many of whom had studied in their respective conservatories before. I had landed up in a drama school with degrees in physics, mathematics and management. There were some more students like myself, but we were a serious minority.

I do not remember having the ease in drama school that many others did. I was not a natural by any measure. I was shy and I was adjusting to a completely new way of life in London. Most importantly, I was not sure what was I doing there. Why I was learning what I was learning.

We were doing exciting things in class which would all qualify as valid theatre training, but I still continued to miss the internal image of anything that I was working on. I was receiving everything, but it was as if nothing was being stored in my body. It was falling off the skin as opposed to getting in.

We did a series of exercises with neutral masks, and most people in my class were immensely moved by the experience. I remember some of my colleagues crying when they took off their masks, but I could not relate to it at all. I was learning craft. How to walk, move, connect to a mask on one's body. This did me a lot of good later on in my practice but at that time it only felt like I was chasing something elusive.

Then two things happened which opened things for me. I hadn't found an answer but definitely a window to what I was looking for.

My friend and housemate Baerbel Aschenberg, who now works for theatre Anu in Germany, introduced me one night to the work of the Polish group Gardzienice. She told me about them, showed me a book and also played a video of their work.

Suddenly, something opened up for me. I saw the semblance of an internal image. An association was in place as this group ran outdoors, made work as a community and said words in their own language.

I owe a lot of my first international exposure to European theatre groups to Baerbel, and this was perhaps one of the earliest groups she introduced me to and easily one of the most significant. The next day in class, while we were improvising, for the first time I said something in Bangla. I had never in my life till the age of twenty-six – through school, college and amateur theatre – said anything on stage in my mother tongue. In fact, most of it had been in English. I should clarify here that English is in no way a second language for someone like me who grew up in cosmopolitan India. We were largely raised in four languages. My languages were English, Hindi and Urdu from social interactions and Bengali from home. These four languages have had an inseparable role to play in my life. In the formation of my thoughts and ideas.

I had, however, never spoken in Bangla on stage because by the time I had started making theatre, an assumption had manifest itself in the cities that modernity presented itself in English. I had become a part of that automatically.

I enjoyed the liberation of Bangla immensely that day, particularly as an actor. I also believed the same could extend to my writing and directing.

That day in school when I finished my improvisation something had changed. Many of my colleagues mentioned this to me. I was not sure what it was, but it felt like it had something to do with language. I thought if I spoke in Bangla somehow I would be closer to my inner image. But there was still no reason for it. I knew I was moved by Gardzienice in a very personal way although they spoke Polish. I think I could tell even then that language was not the answer but just the beginning of an answer. That if I just switched to my mother tongue I would not find what was missing because what I was looking for was something far more complex and yet far more fundamental.

The second incident that opened the door was directly related to returning home.

Between my two years at LISPA, I had to come back to India. I was in London on a scholarship which covered a year of school. The only other scholarship that could cover my second year could be applied for only if I was back in India. I came back disappointed because I had to leave my peers, who would all complete their programme now without me. There was also no real way of knowing if I would receive the second scholarship or not.

However, this year turned out to be one of the most vital years of my life. I spent a part of this year with some eminent masters of Indian theatre who had worked with traditional forms in order to find a modern language. I had the opportunity to spend time first with Veenapani Chawla of Adishakti Theatre in Pondicherry and then with Heisnam Kanhailal of Kalakshetra theatre in Manipur. They had worked with folk and classical forms to create contemporary theatre pieces. I sat in their rehearsal rooms and workshops, and discussed at length with them about their process. These conversations and rehearsals were very enriching and at the same time partly frustrating because I had no access to any of those traditional forms. In fact, some of the folk and classical forms were even further away from me than what I was learning at LISPA. These works across classical and folk forms of India intrigued me. They taught me an enormous amount of craft. They also taught me to think about theatre while making it. However, I was nowhere close to my inner image. I had nothing particular that could be identified as Indian about me. I was not born into any particular art form.

In the midst of this, one day on a train, I was reading Anne Bogart's book *A Director Prepares*. I was travelling to a school in rural Rajasthan, a state in the western part of India, to conduct a theatre-based training for teachers. I was extremely occupied with the question of this inner image. This was also the time I was about to start directing my new play, *Lucknow '76*, which was about the rule of Queen Victoria in 1876 and the Indian Emergency imposed by Indira Gandhi in 1976. It is a play I had researched and written while I was in London and dealt with two parallel narratives about censorship and rule by power. The play was set in the city of Lucknow in North India, a place with a rich cultural and historical heritage. In my childhood, I had spent a significant amount of time there and, hence, had very vivid images and experiences of the place. I did not, however, have an internal image of the play as yet.

Here I was, recently returned from London and travelling through Rajasthan as I yearned for an answer to my play set in Lucknow, reading a book by an American director facing a similar crisis of understanding what her tradition was as she workshopped in Germany!

And Anne Bogart wrote the most important thing about tradition I had ever read. That she realized that although she was American, a child of a naval officer who had travelled everywhere, she too had some traditions. She did not have an ancient form, but she had nonetheless access to vaudeville, black-and-white films and other forms of performances she had seen and heard as a child. That in a way these were her inner-scape and her tradition.

This blew my mind. It was so incredibly simple and yet so true for my own condition. In fact, I had had so much access to tradition myself without noticing it. In India, even the most modern form is a few hundred years old. So, in fact, I had something deep to access. And that day on that train to a rural school, an American director gave me an answer which led me to think more closely about what is tradition in the first place and what did I have.

It also made me suddenly recognize that when I was with masters of Indian theatre like Heisnam Kanhailal and Veenapani Chawla, I was actually very close to my internal image. I thought their work was about transforming something technically. But actually, they too were ultimately chasing their inner pictures, and those pictures could not be made by one form of tradition or one view of modernity alone. Hence, in fact, their own quest was filled with pluralities.

In India there are so many layers to a person's existence, merely in terms of the number of traditions that compose her day-to-day life, that it would be juvenile to try to find just one strand to exclusively call one's own. This identification is useful for marketing companies and festival brochures but has no real bearing on one's actual process. We do not live in a single timeline. Within a kilometre it is possible in any Indian city to find a thirteenth-century Hindu temple, a seventeenth-century mosque, a procession that deals with a folklore from the third century and even large billboards advertising the next major technological breakthrough.

This coexistence of images, sounds, ideas and histories shapes our inner images.

This, I believe, is true for many places in the world and particularly cosmopolitan cities. In fact, the entire 'New World' from the mid-1800s is full of people like us. Children of migrants from the Old World who arrived somewhere to survive the traumas of colonization, partitions, world wars and subsequent decolonization. People like us can be found from Australia to the Caribbean islands if one travels east to west. There are hardly any people who have stayed where they originated from. There is hardly any identity that is now stable and singular across three generations of an ethnicity.

There is, in fact, a deeper ramification to what Anne Bogart says that goes beyond the practical aspect of looking for one's roots.

It is that *tradition is not ethnicity*.

My sister and I have the same ethnicity but could belong to completely different traditions due to the particular slice of the New World we have had the agency or interest to participate in.

Tradition in art, that inner image, has nothing to do in a way with one's mother tongue, ethnic music, food habits or religious belief.

It is something much deeper and more complex.

I think tradition in art is that series of images or sounds that one is perpetually seeking because these are the formative mix that shaped one's mind when one was very young.

It is perpetually possible to develop these into different forms through the use of the relevant craft or tool. It is not a fixed monolith. Not something that has an objective reality. But something that shapes the subjective experience of the artist.

The tradition itself can be an image of solitude from one's childhood, or it can be a grand performance that takes a month to complete and is attended by thousands of people. It can be a form of singing or a form of reprimand. One way to understand one's tradition is to list all these images from one's formative years and then try to unpack what these images and sounds are made of.

In this way the tradition of a modern cosmopolitan artist is inextricably linked to memory. This is also the only tradition I think one can rely on because art is ultimately a way of remembering the future. It happens now, but it always creates the past in the next moment. Our subconscious is filled with these mixed images and sounds rather than neat compartments of forms and techniques. It is crucial for an artist to differentiate between life and its representation.

II

My earliest memory of watching theatre comprises three kinds of theatre I had early access to.

The first is the Garhwali Ramlila, which is a performance of *Ramayana* in the language of Garhwal (a region of Uttarakhand, one of the mountain states of India).

I grew up in a university campus where every year this Ramlila was performed by many people from Garhwal who were also clerks, peons and drivers. One of my most vivid memories is that of a driver who used to become a god for this time. I remember how he would become god on the stage and then exit to chat and smoke with everyone, and then go back to being a god with the next entry as if his godhood was uninterrupted. This used to be played in a makeshift open-air space and would often last all night. Everyone knew the story, and it just kept playing during the holy month of the Hindus when it is believed that Rama returns from Lanka (nothing to do with Sri Lanka of today) to his hometown in North India in the epic. The university would be abuzz with the talk of the Ramlila. It used to become part of everyone's lives for some time. The images from this Ramlila that we used to attend sometimes – the people watching it, the hawkers selling things around it and my sister's hands holding me in the crowd – are definitely part of my tradition.

The second form was in the rehearsals of the great Indian theatre director Habib Tanvir. Habib 'Sahab' (as he was called by the adults) used to sometimes rehearse in a part of our university and my father took me to watch his rehearsal a few times. Habib Tanvir had quit RADA to backpack across Europe and stayed on for some time in Brecht's Berliner Ensemble. He was completely taken up by the politics and formal ideas of the Ensemble. He came back to India and gave up English theatre to work with actors of a folk form called Nacha in the language of his native region of Chhattisgarh.

Nacha is a highly improvised form but Habib Tanvir brought great structure and modern dramaturgy into its freedom. This invigorated both Nacha and the modern stories he wanted to tell. His way of directing is etched in my mind. The most fascinating thing about his work was the sheer audacity of it. Habib Tanvir's theatre group, Naya Theatre (new theatre), was not loyal to any one form or reverential to anything. They were, in fact, the opposite of the classical arts but they dealt with classical subjects of moral complexities and the like very often. The most analogous to a Western audience would probably be the theatre of Dario Fo.

The third form was Bangla plays that my much older cousins performed as part of their theatre group Dhumketu in Delhi and also other Bangla plays that we saw during the Bengali festival of Durga Pujo.

Bengali theatre had already in the 1980s found several strands of modernity. It was in itself a hybrid of rural and suburban forms such as Jatra (an open-air theatre in the round) and the upper-middle-class proscenium theatre of Calcutta. Also, Bengal has had a very strong left movement and hence a large part of its theatre was a mix of these three influences.

Even today, I love Bengali theatre. Even the worst most unbearable productions. It is like comfort food for me. I have seen some extraordinary Bengali theatre and some really terrible works too. However, I do not watch Bengali theatre in the same way as I watch other theatre. For me, it is a place to rest.

Ramlila, Habib Tanvir and the Bengali theatre that I saw are very clearly part of my theatre tradition, although from the outside one may not find many similarities in them. They can seem like completely different propositions. It is only my experience with them that binds them to make a clear cohesive tradition.

Later on, as I grew up, I saw the work of Sunil Shanbagh, who works in Hindi. Sunil's work is in a way the most perfect metamorphosis I have seen of these three sources of my own tradition. Sunil remains the closest director I can attribute my work directly to.

He himself comes from a tradition of a very important director of urban amateur theatre, Satyadev Dubey. Dubey worked in both Marathi and Hindi theatre and is responsible for staging many new plays, which are now classics of contemporary drama, by working with new writers with very limited resources. In a way, I think my entire theatre work is a straight line from Dubey, although I met him only once as he rarely worked outside Bombay.

I also saw the theatre of Neelam Mansingh Chowdhry. Her scenography, use of colour, texture and elements from the village life of her native Punjab, is etched in my mind. I attribute her scenography and Sunil's direction as my most direct influences. However, I still think what I can call as my tradition rolls back to those three earliest forms.

When I make theatre anywhere in the world, in any language, in any form, I ask myself what would be the Garhwali Ramlila version of this. I immediately form an inner image of the play. I get a sense of what it should do to people who are watching it. At what distance should the audience be and how should the performance be pitched. I have never used anything of the Garhwali Ramlila as it is but I use its pulse. I use what it reminds me of today. With every passing year, as I get older, I realize I also remember the Ramlila differently.

I also ask myself how would Habib Tanvir do this and find again a mishmash of answers that root me to an approach.

Finally, I cannot escape the Bengali theatre. I have had the opportunity to direct at some of the most beautiful theatres in the world and also direct street performances that play in markets and factories. To me, always, I imagine a boy in the audience who is sitting with his sister and watching this play. The codes, the tone, pitch, the politics need to work for that boy.

I should clarify here that I have never directed anything that looks anything remotely close to the theatre traditions that I mention. At least not consciously. However, this image is not for the audience. This image is for me. It is the image on which everything will be built.

Heisnam Kanhailal had once told me that the West has the ability to convert forms of exercise into theatre exercises. About how Grotowski had converted Yoga to actual theatre exercises, but our drama schools failed to do so outside of Badal Sircar. He said that our problem is that we teach Yoga, Kalarippayattu and other physical forms separately and then hope that the actor will miraculously synthesize them into performance. He said that modernity was about being able to convert tradition into theatre that works for the subject at hand.

This has stayed with me in a big way.

Whenever I am writing or directing a new work for any theatre in the world, I first try to find out: What does it do? What am I entering? What is the contract between that theatre and its community? What forms does it engage in and what could be the tradition that it sits inside?

Theatre is an extremely contextual act. Its ability to be able to touch a chord with human beings universally is so deeply located that its artifice necessarily needs to be extremely specific. Every single person in the audience watches a different play. Yet everyone has a theatre building or theatre tradition they go to more often than others.

People can watch films from around the world in any theatre. They can read a book from anywhere sitting in any place. However, even when they do watch a play from anywhere in the world, most of the time they watch it in the same building. Theatre is a form deeply entrenched in its space. Time is what we experience in the theatre but space is the real context. We watch the same production completely differently if we watch it in a different theatre. In fact, we watch it differently even if the approach road and the foyer of the theatre we regularly pass through changes.

Theatre buildings are like the local post office, where letters from around the world arrive but a person we know for years delivers it. If a new person delivers the letter, we feel differently about opening it.

This is a delicate dance.

Whenever I make a play for a theatre, I want to understand their tradition to some degree. I want to then be part of the tradition but inexplicably it will be changed because I will come with my own tradition, my limitations, my imperfections and audacities.

The exercise of two people from different traditions meeting each other is only useful, in my opinion, if both traditions change ever so slightly by this production. If they don't, it is death. Boring. Stale theatre. For a play to be alive in the context of the meeting of traditions, a new formal language needs to be evolved.

If an audience can look at a production and say that this was a 'musical with a monologue and a folk performance along with an Ibsen text', the play is dead. The audience must receive a whole, no matter how many disparate elements come together to make the play. There is no place for reductionism when attempting to create something outside of the comfort of a single tradition.

In fact, this is also the greatest difficulty with arts-funding agencies in the world. What they ask for more often than not are all the wrong questions.

The language of modernity and experiment in most arts-funding agencies is terribly reductive and downright lazy. Theatre is not made in that way. It is not made by adding forms, it is made by transcending memory. Tradition is not inherently formal, although it might be made up of a conglomeration of forms. It is not puppetry plus chorus plus ritual. It is the feeling of fear plus the colour yellow plus the feeling of touching my sister's hand. No funding agency will dare to fund a proposal that outlines feelings and memory. However, formal reductionism often receives support due to the inability of arts-funding organizations at spending adequate amount of time and energy on what the artist actually wants to say.

At the same time, art is about craft. It is a practical thing. It is not magic. It is not about genius or inspiration. Especially as a director, where one works and solves problems. These problems are solved by doing very specific things with time and space.

A director can walk into the room with thousands of internal images, but it has to ultimately be translated to specific doable things.

Everyone in the rehearsal room has their own internal image of the play. It is the ability to work with everyone's internal image while continuing to make one's own hotter and more urgent that makes a good director effective. A director must remember that the reason all these people are in the room is that no one image is enough (including their own), and yet to achieve a coherent whole everyone needs to be steered to explore their images with a set of common parameters.

This steering requires technique. And technique can come from anywhere.

I use an enormous lot of what I learnt in drama school in my rehearsal. I use commedia dell'arte, clown and buffoon to direct plays which from the outside look nothing like any of these forms. However, what my drama school in London gave me was a toolkit and the recognition of the importance of an objective eye.

Sometimes I'm in rehearsal with actors from completely different backgrounds. One has trained in a traditional art form, the other in a Western physical theatre form and the third in method. One is from a small town, the other from a village and the third from a big city, and in no particular order.

To be able to work in such a diverse group one must 'convert tradition to theatre exercises'. One must find something to *do* which takes us beyond our articulate differences. Something to *do* is very important if one really needs to find out what is the tradition of this room.

I devised an engine when I was in the second year of drama school. Maybe this was a remnant of my physics days. An engine that could generate exercises as one needs in rehearsal. I owe this as much to what I learnt from Kanhailal and Veenapani as I do to LISPA.

It's a simple model in which you fix three elements and keep discovery as your goal in rehearsal.

Then this is repeated in different combinations to arrive at a staging idea or a form or to unpack and mine a scene.

The three components are:

1. Objective
2. Constraint
3. Stage time, or play time.

So, for instance, if we need to devise an exercise that helps us stage the first meeting between Hamlet and his father's ghost, I would say to the room that we are going to try an improvisation as follows:

1. Objective: To stage an unexpected meeting
2. Constraint: The entire scene will be in song
3. Stage time, or play time: The improvisation lasts for ten minutes and the scene is about an entire night.

This improvisation might give us only a minute of stage time, if it works really well. This is on a good day.

Now let us assume that we discovered that there is a moment in which the ghost seems to be falling off the ramparts of the fort. It feels like a moment when the ghost will die!

This also means it's an opportunity to save his father.

We could now build the next improvisation as follows:

1. Objective: To save the father's ghost
2. Constraint: We should be able to see the image from Munch's painting *The Scream*
3. Stage time, or play time: The improvisation lasts for ten minutes and the moment is actually about twenty seconds long.

I often find that the advantage of this exercise is that actors from completely different traditions find a way of negotiating their differences by focusing on these specifics without having to lose their individuality. It gives us a method that acts as a language to make discoveries in rehearsal.

In places like London, Berlin and New York, actors often have a common language because they have been through similar training. However, in most other places where actors could come from completely different kinds of training, one has to find a common language first in rehearsal.

This 'engine', so to speak, has held me in good stead in many places. I was once leading a workshop in a theatre in Freiburg, in which we had two actors from India, two from the German repertory of a Romanian theatre and, also, actors from Burkina Faso. In the first fifteen minutes, one could tell that this is a rich room but with completely varying traditions that people come from.

An exercise like this helps to give everyone very concretely something to do together.

No modern play can rest on one form. We simply do not have the luxury of traditional forms wherein the code is taught from a young age and everyone knows the code.

A traditional form is known for its virtuosity of being able to repeat itself with variation.

A modern play is known for re-finding the form itself and generating a form for the play in rehearsal.

In my opinion, unless there is a discovery of a form, a modern play is cosmetic.

For it to come alive, the audience and the players need to go through the anticipation of form. It is an extraordinary encounter in a theatre when the play and the audience are arriving at the moment when enough time has passed and motifs have reappeared for the form to make sense. The content of the play is absolutely crucial but it is this anticipation that we all carry inside us when we listen to a story.

Great stories have this ability to keep us wrapped in their spells by delaying our satisfaction with form. They keep us hanging and yet release security in doses.

In the *Arabian Nights*, we are always aware of the larger structure in which Scheherazade has to keep telling stories. However, the structure within the stories is completely different every time and it is here that the greatness of the book lies.

Children listen to the same story night after night because they have the mythical ability to live in this moment. Hence, to be able to anticipate the same thing over and over again.

As we grow older, we get ahead of ourselves. Our traditions become solidified. Fossilize and cease to remain traditions anymore. If it is dead, then it is not a tradition.

Some years ago, I made a discovery while watching a play in London. I think it was a production of Lorraine Hansberry's *Les Blancs* at the National Theatre. At various points, I felt that the audience seemed hugely familiar. Its reactions, its sighs and screams were something I had seen and heard before. A few months later, I had the same experience in New York City while watching a production of *Odyssey* at the Public.

I was thinking about this similarity while on a ferry crossing over to Staten island, when I realized that actually all audiences in the world are always watching two plays. They are watching the play on stage and they are watching the *Mahabharata*.

They may or may not know this, of course.

But I believe that subconsciously we go to theatre to watch the *Mahabharata*. A story in which there will be hundreds of archetypes and yet each one different from the other. The characters will go through all possible emotions of human beings and ask profound questions. They will also depict the most mundane behaviour while asking these questions. In the end, there will be a war (or any event) that all of us knew will happen but secretly did not want to happen. We would also feel terribly cheated if it did not. Finally, the lines of good and evil will blur. A protagonist and his family will go to an eternal mountain led by an ordinary dog. The heroes will become ordinary and the gods will be punished and worshipped at the same time.

I believe very strongly that my tradition has given me this story, but so has everyone else's tradition given them this story by different names.

There is only this story to tell, hear and watch. Everyone has their own Mahabharata.

My tradition calls it by the name of *Mahabharata*. Other people's traditions have given them their own 'super-story', a narrative and image that contains all the other stories by which they can examine the world.

This super-story is an extremely crucial marker of our tradition, and it is not on the brochure, poster, reviews or trailers but it is running inside us.

When I am unable to move forward with a scene in my rehearsal room, I ask myself which scene of the *Mahabharata* would this be.

No one else knows this because they are watching their own *Mahabharata*. They are here to try to understand why are we here, what should we do here and where will we go after this life, except that they have their own tradition of storytelling and stories that they have come with.

For others it is their epic story. It might be the story of Adam, Gilgamesh, Christ, *Arabian Nights* or the *Shahnama* of Iran, but all of us deeply have these stories inside us.

In the meeting of my *Mahabharata* and their traditions of stories, a new tradition is created and both our traditions are transformed forever.

It is this new production that will someday form the basis of someone else's tradition. They will have the same experience I had with the Garhwali Ramlila, the Bangla theatre or Habib Tanvir, if our work is any good. They will push the wheel of tradition forward and the tradition of theatre will keep evolving to find new meanings and new languages. Through these discoveries, every artist will also keep finding what is really their own tradition. And they will recognize that the only way of living in one's tradition is to meet others' traditions.

2

Language of theatre

I

Language of words and music: An early language

I grew up in a house full of words and music. My parents were both bibliophiles. They read in Bengali, Hindi and English. Our house was full of books in all three languages and since we lived in a university campus, our life was surrounded with the presence of books and avid readers.

The other major presence in our house was that of Hindustani classical and Bengali music. Every evening, my mother's Guru and the other students would assemble in our living room and practice their singing. For hours I would hear these songs and elaborations of ragas in our house. I recognized these two forms of language, that of words and music, as major ingredients of my life very early on at home.

We also saw theatre in many languages. Some of this theatre invariably had a lot of music and movement, whereas some others would be in the mode of European realism that avoided the formal musical elaborations unlike traditional Indian forms. However, deep down, I think I was aware of the musicality of both kinds of theatre. I had always found that any performance that I admired was musically satisfying irrespective of whether it actually had music or not. The stories and forms were deeply connected to the language they were performed in, and the myths and tales that these plays presented were unique to their language. Garhwali (a north-

Indian language from the mountains), Chhattisgarhi (a language from central India), Hindi and Bengali had distinctly different theatre forms. Some languages had developed plays as rituals and community performances, whereas some others, due to their connection with urbanity, had developed both classical Indian and European realist idioms. There seemed to be little to no osmosis between these forms of theatre, and it truly felt like watching completely different modes of expression in each language.

I could not obviously articulate this at that age but I am quite certain of noticing this early. The fact that language in theatre had a function of providing context, communicating the story and that of musicality was something, I believe, I was inherently aware of at an early age.

One of the key ideas I received from home was that 'language is culture'. It contains within it codes that people speak to each other in. It contains the music of that culture. It contains the rise and fall of its fate in history. It tells us how insular a culture has been and who have been its allies. It tells us who conquered the people who speak this language, and it tells us what is the history of shame, pride and guilt in it. A language also tells us if a dramatic culture expects those it is performing to primarily hear (audience, from audio), watch (*darshak*, Hindi word for viewer), appreciate (*prekshak*, Hindi word for one who understands the art and can critically appreciate) or play together (*khelaghar*, Bangla word for the room in which people play).

From home, I learnt early on that to fully appreciate any form of theatre, or art in general, it was important to understand its codes, history, symbols – in other words, its context – and its music. My mother read music in both Western and Bengali *swaralipi* notation. She sang Hindustani classical music and seamlessly moved to the organ in our house to play Western chords for songs by the poet and composer Rabindranath Tagore. Thinking about her practice, I see a seamless existence of an artist in both worlds of her art form because of her comfort and understanding of both contexts. She was very keen that we understand the context of what we were reading, watching and listening, providing us all the context to be able to appreciate the different kinds of art we were in contact with.

Growing up, I realized that receiving the context is not always a given, but there are ways and means to find a way in. Sometimes the access to the context is given to us at birth and sometimes we collaborate with people who have access to it. In both cases, the material must be first internalized over a period of time and the word is, in fact, the last step to arrive at.

This understanding helped me enormously later on in life to make theatre across different languages, contexts and geographies. The formulation was provided at home.

II

The arrival of English

English arrived in school. Like many other urban Indians, I went to an English-medium school. In a way that has known to be a ticket to a larger world for a long time in our country. However, our relationship to English was restricted to school books and the instructions by teachers in class. Outside of class work, all interactions were in Hindustani (Hindi and Urdu) with my peers and in Bangla with my family. My parents were very particular that at home we spoke in Bangla, especially because we were growing up in Delhi which is by and large a Hindi-speaking place.

When we moved out of our university campus to a more upper-middle-class locality, suddenly we had to speak in English in our day-to-day lives. My sister and I took many lessons from our mother in dealing with the failure to speak this language correctly.

We saw her fail, correct herself and speak again with great dignity. We were supported by her to not feel ashamed of her or our own inabilities. This also taught us that any language can be learnt, and that it gets better with use. One need not feel ashamed of oneself while learning it and that one's body changes with each new language.

By the time I was thirteen, my school had become extremely strict about the use of the English language. It introduced a new rule by which children who spoke in Hindi were to be fined one rupee per word. Every row in our class was assigned a 'monitor', whose work was to watch out for students who failed to speak in English with each other. Students had to report this behaviour about each other. One of my closest friends who was from a household in which no one spoke English would give the class monitor fifty rupees in the beginning of the week so that he could breathe easy in class!

Ngũgĩ wa Thiong'o writes in his book *Decolonising the Mind* about the same phenomenon in Nigeria in his childhood. He describes it as a way of instilling the feeling of doubt in the community, where suddenly people start to report each other. In a colonial context, Thiong'o makes this extraordinary point about how language destroys solidarities of the oppressed. In our childhood, a few decades after Thiong'o's, neocolonialism was taking shape using many of the same techniques. My school, in fact, was quite progressive. It was run by the Tagore Education Trust and, as a result, had many of its principles of education derived from the thoughts of the great Indian poet after whom the trust was named, Rabindranath Tagore, the first Asian to win the Nobel Prize in literature. Tagore was also a pedagogue and had founded an extremely interesting international school in Bengal, the Shanti Niketan. Tagore's own school, I am sure, did not have this emphasis on English. Our school, on the other hand, being in Delhi had the foresight to see that in the future to come, being able to speak in English would be the single most distinguishing factor.

This was the first time in my life that I had connected language to power.

It is also around this time that our mother took my sister and me to watch our first professional English play. In a plush auditorium in Delhi, we went to see a production of *My Fair Lady*. Victor Banerjee, an acclaimed Bengali actor, was playing the role of Henry Higgins.

We had seen many plays before but out here the difference was clear right from the entrance. There were young women dressed up as servers in a British household serving hot cross buns! It was the first time I had seen what these buns really were, although there were English rhymes and poems I had learnt as a child that spoke of them. The performances were extraordinary, the music was brilliant and I will never forget the moment in which Victor Banerjee missed some lines and requested the sound technician to go back a bit and play again.

The anticipation of that error being rectified in our presence was a truly theatrical moment.

I loved the play. I went back home enamoured by it. In any case, I loved most live performances that I was taken to and this had been really special and novel.

However, what was firmly established above everything else is that this was really the glamorous theatre of Delhi. That this is what high society did in the evening and hence, this was the culture of the elite.

With the fine-system in school and this posh production, I had for the first time learnt that language is intrinsically connected to not just context and music but also power.

Gradually through the 1990s, every aspect of life around me changed to English rapidly. Cable television brought to people's homes English channels. English cinema played in more halls and in my generation, an entire urban middle-class milieu moved away from Indian languages to exclusively English music. By the time I was in university, a lot of the upper-middle-class theatre was in English. I really enjoyed Hindi and Bangla theatre, but its space had diminished. If anyone from my generation and background engaged in theatre, it was by and large in English. It performed great texts, it had the costumes, the money, the lighting – but something about it always struck false to me. I stayed away from it and gradually the theatre itself took a back seat for me. I did not know what was it about the English theatre in Delhi at that time that felt so drab and boring to me. As a result, I moved away and in my university days had almost nothing to do with making theatre.

III

The language of theatre

Delhi gets extremely hot in summers with temperatures rising to mid-forties. My college was some distance away and often, while moving around the city, one needed respite from the scorching heat.

Abhimanch, the auditorium of National School of Drama (NSD), was one of the cheapest places to sit in an air-conditioned hall, and it was on the route to my college. Many a times when they would stage their repertory plays, I would get a ticket and sit inside for the air conditioning. For twenty rupees, this was great value for money. The longer the play, the better. More time in the air-conditioned room.

NSD staged its plays in Hindi and its repertory included some of the hallmark plays of Indian theatre. I knew nothing about the plays it staged but as I dealt with the summer, I got more and more enamoured by what I saw. It is here in Abhimanch, in the moments of these beautiful accidents, that I learnt what was missing in the English theatre. In the Hindi theatre, even in its most classical versions, wherein I knew even lesser words than those in English plays, there was a clear theatrical language. A language that went way beyond the spoken one. This theatre had synthesized the physical, visual and aural languages of the play.

Hindi theatre, like the Bangla theatre, not only staged the best of playwrights from around the world but also had found a consistent body and visual framing for the actor, who could then present a language that was greater than the sum of its parts. It had codes, history and secrets. The English theatre of that time, on the other hand, was by and large aping what some of its actors and directors had seen in the West. The actors had no body to carry those words. The stage was a poor copy of something that had not emerged from any roots. Even internationally acclaimed directors such as Fritz Bennewitz came to NSD and worked in Hindi. The institution itself has a complicated history of hegemonizing Hindi over all the other languages of India, thereby not providing actors of non-Hindi-speaking backgrounds equal opportunities for major roles as others. Nonetheless, the productions in its repertory were created bottom-up. The body, the context, the rhythms, design and understanding of the actor were prepared to discover the language of the text.

I hold this lesson from those days at Abhimanch theatre very dearly even today. I have worked in many languages in India and internationally, and while directing, I actually arrive at the spoken word in rehearsal quite late in the process. We tend to spend a lot of time preparing the ground for the world with actors who have lived in that language. I do not believe that theatrical language is devoid of the spoken word language. Even in a silent play like Ōta Shōgo's *The Water Station*, in which people walk across stage with no words and at an extremely slow pace to get to a place of respite, the presence of the Japanese language looms over.

Spoken word does not need to be spoken on stage. It exists in the way people walk. The art of the theatre is fundamentally non-reductive. The stage is a place where the spoken, the physical and the visual merge in a seamless unison. This unity needs to be created through rehearsal with great patience and care.

As a director, my primary job is to prepare the roots. Not to be obsessed with the fruits or flowers. A theatre-maker who works across languages and cultures must carry with them the tools to make a theatrical language sow its seeds in the early days of rehearsal. One of my heroes, Asheem Chakravarty, a musician I admired immensely growing up, used to say that a composer is like a gardener and an arranger is like the florist. One is growing the plant and the other is making the bouquet. This distinction is extremely vital while making this kind of cross-cultural work. Else, it runs the risk of shopping for form. The easiest thing in this world is to put on a show. One can go to ten places, pick up all kinds of music, forms and costumes that exoticize and entertain, and then place them next to each other by using the most elementary instinct of composition. A simple rise and fall of tempo can see this kind of thing through. However, this can only take us to the theatre of appeasement. That only pleases through novelty. No art should take on that role. The most facile form of entertainment is one that has lost its confidence in its own language. Which uses only the sense of wonder to keep audiences engaged. It does nothing for society except celebrating the status quo.

In fact, I respectfully disagree with Peter Brook when he says one should not bore people in the theatre. I do not think boredom is a problem. We can bore people. We need to promise an inner journey through the boredom. In fact, I think that in today's world of overstimulation, it is absolutely compulsory to find moments of boredom in a play. It is the bridge that connects novelty to reflection. Without this bridge of boredom, we would never be able to make that transition from awe to reflection in our lives. The boredom has to be meaningful. That is all.

A director who works in different contexts and languages must create exercises, conversations, curations and invite such guests into the rehearsal room who can create the fertile ground on which a language of theatre can develop. This is far less work when one is in a traditional set-up. A Ramlila (the story of Rama performed in many traditional theatrical traditions of northern India) or a Bengali Jatra play is already firmly set in codes and context. Its challenge is to engage with modernity. It knows its audiences are ever-changing. For reasons of religious proselytizing or crass commerce, it needs to continuously innovate. The risk of ossification lies with high-art. That which plays to predetermined small elite circles, which treat the language of theatre not unlike the language of greeting, simply as a tool of social value.

Many years after my NSD theatre watching days, I was reminded of the magic of a well-developed theatrical language while watching a production of Tadashi Suzuki's *The Trojan Women* in Yokohama. In a little theatre, I saw a no-frills production that explored the enormous human cost of war. There were no extraordinary lights, set or sound effects. The text was completely in Japanese. On one hand, the theatrical language went way beyond the spoken word, and on the other, it never became a physical form outside of the sound and shape of Japanese language. It was not just a series of staging devices that removed the argument from the staging. It is precisely because the production tied in the relationship between the spoken language and the non-spoken theatrical language that it had its profound impact on so many of us who were not Japanese speakers.

IV

Multilingualism and multiculturalism

Being multilingual means different things in different places. In India, being multilingual is a natural state. It is not good or bad, superior or inferior, to any other culture, but it is just a reality of our country. It is, in some ways, a great gift that many people have access to different ideas, thoughts and literatures because of this inherent multilingualism.

In India, multilingualism is also inherently multicultural. We are inherently a linguistically divided country with our division of states being on linguistic grounds post-independence. Every language group has its own rituals, customs, food habits, versions of epics and distinct lifestyles.

Although this may seem common sense, a little enquiry into multilingual spaces can lead us to see that multilingualism and multiculturalism may not necessarily follow. One can very easily be in the duty-free zone in an airport where despite a huge multilingual diversity the culture is essentially the same. On the other hand, one can walk into the Grand Bazaar in Istanbul and notice how although most people speak the same language, there are completely different cultures at play.

This distinction is extremely important for a theatre-maker to consider while deciding on the language and approach to a play. It is extremely easy to mix up the two ideas or to consider them to be in service of the same idea everywhere, thereby making colossal cultural blunders.

Several well-known directors have attempted to create multilingual productions assuming that the form will stand in for diversity. However, many of these have ended up creating a monoculture inside the play.

The challenge with creating multilingual theatre remains the same as it is with productions in one language: to find the language bottom-up. The body of the actor, the codes of the culture(s), the history, the music have to be developed in rehearsal in order to arrive at the multilingualism. Predetermined multilingualism can lead to the entire theatre-making exercise becoming a game of charades. The objective of the piece can very easily slip into a proof of universality. That we roughly understand what Actor A is saying to Actor B in Polish and what Actor B's response is in Hindi and then Actor C's in Flemish. The success of the production thus depends on our ability to guess what they have said. The production can waste too much of its time and resources in rehearsal playing this game and congratulating itself on the success of it determining humanist universals. This is only worth it if the production has found a new language which can hold on its own. However, if the play is only a collection of languages and bodies, it is like presenting one's grocery bag and not sharing a piece of art.

A director who works across cultures and languages must remember that exciting devices used in rehearsal that unlock potentials of the play are not the play. That icebreakers are not theatre. There has to be solid reason that one needs to arrive at in order to have a form in the play.

In classical Indian drama, plays had more than one language. The reason was that different castes spoke different languages. When I wrote *Muktidham* (The Salvation House) in 2017, a play set in eighth-century India, I had to write five kinds of Hindi in it to mirror that reality. However, in *Kaumudi* (Moonlight) that I wrote in 2014, which deals with themes of theatre and the *Mahabharata*,

I have lost an opportunity to mirror differences of culture across caste using differences in language.

I once made a nine-part play about the women in *Mahabharata* with actresses from different parts of the world. We had a Hebrew-speaking mother who frets over her sons with a completely different cultural presence compared to a Cantonese-speaking mother who let her sons go. The two actresses, Yarit Dor in Hebrew and Janice Im in Cantonese, brought their different cultural readings of the texts to the rehearsal room. I had to not interfere. My job as a director was, in fact, to stay out. To create the room where many ideas could grow and then in the end keep focusing on the roots and pointing at what was being developed.

A harder more rigid idea would have destroyed this piece.

In this piece on the *Mahabharata* in nine different languages, we actually managed a multicultural view with multilingualism in the form. However, while in *Kaumudi* where we do have three to four different Hindis, it remains monocultural at one level because the caste dimension has been errantly ignored in the linguistic politics of the play.

V

Internationalism and theatrical language

A play set in eighth-century India could work quite well in India in any Indian language. The classical nature of the play can be found in the spoken, visual and physical culture of both Sanskrit and Dravidian languages, which are respectively roots of the northern and southern families of languages of India for most parts. If this play, however, was done in English in India, it would ring extremely false. This is because one does not relate the English language with the bodies, costumes, gait, shape or form of that time.

In the United States or the United Kingdom, however, if the play is staged in English, audiences may come out of the theatre having gained an enriching experience without a problem. This is because they have nothing to compare this production with.

However, I do feel that if audiences in the West could see international work in their original language with supertitles, they would have a much richer experience than watching them in

English. Again, this has less to do with just the spoken language. It is about the kind of detail an actor of another language can bring to the stories of their world. It is about the pausing, gait, breath and gestures. One cannot find the dramatic language of a culture without extending oneself to include the spoken language of that culture.

It would be unthinkable for people to walk into a film festival at the Southbank Centre in London and watch multiple screenplays of the world performed on screen uniformly in English with actors from London. However, this is exactly where international programming stands in major theatre centres such as London and New York. If five theatres in New York and London took it upon themselves to stage all their international work in the original language for three years, I think the expectation from international work would forever be changed.

Actors of non-white backgrounds in these places are also trapped in this false premise. They are forever dealing in 'Indian accents' and 'Arab looks' on their resume, as if there was any such homogenous category in the real world. By creating this false market of international work with British and American actors – who are supremely talented, many of whom I love and who have been some of my best collaborators – theatres in these Anglophilic countries are denying both audiences and actors of authentic work. The actors have to wait for plays to come from their great-grandfather's countries to get meaty parts. Why the prince of Denmark can be a white guy from Sheffield but not a brown man from Eastham is anyone's guess. If we can believe that a little room in the basement of a theatre is Elsinore, it should not take much to believe that the man with the Urdu accent can be the young prince.

In my view, international work right now is way behind non-international work. This is mainly because dramaturgy departments believe that if you have a translation, the job is done. They believe that the language of theatre can continue to be British, American, German or French, as long as the play has been translated into their language. They do not understand or put in the effort to understand that the root of the choices in a play from Syria, India or Lebanon comes from considerations of theatrical conventions and theatre language. They do not come from the spoken word alone. And they do not come from the translator's language at all.

Directors who create work internationally absolutely must invest long hours and years in trying to engage with the world they are making the work about and for. In my view, a play is only valid if it holds in its place of origin, no matter what language it is in.

Every young theatre-maker in the world today who is going to work outside of their own context is going to have to face the challenge of finding the right theatre language for their work. It is important to recognize that the answer can be more complex today than simply making the prince of Denmark speak in English or asking actors from around the world to perform the *Mahabharata* in English. These are experiments of a time when theatre-makers made theatre in one context over a long period of time and developed methods for that context alone. Today, it is important to recognize that one will have to find solutions for each production and context.

When I am working on a street play in Delhi about caste-politics, I have to write three kinds of Hindi to suit each caste's position and its voice. But while writing an English play about Tibet, which is to be performed in translation in Tibetan, should I be writing different kinds of English? While directing Romanian actors in a theatre in Germany, I cannot dream of using the same metaphors for creating the piece as I would use in New York. While working with dancers in Yokohama, I cannot think about the body in the same way as I would while working with a dancer in Brazil. I have to find out the specifics of each context and each collaboration.

We spend days in rehearsal staging scenes of birth, death, separation and meeting without any context of predetermined language. We often go through multiple rounds of workshops to develop the dramatic language(s) that are contained in this particular ensemble for this particular context in this room. I am, of course, presupposing here that the ensemble is diverse and a good representation of the world we are trying to build. We create close to a hundred moments of these essential themes using song, movement, rhythm, sounds, dance and stillness in a few weeks. These physical and aural moments give us the basis of creating the work ahead. This is where the theatrical language is developed from.

On the other hand, we also improvise on specifics. A moment where a woman from Beijing meets a Tibetan man in the middle of a riot is completely different from the meeting of a Kashmiri man and a North-Indian soldier. The codes of danger, the words of disgust or rebuke, the anxieties are all culture-specific. These cannot be created using principles of false universalism.

Today, theatre-makers like myself work in no one industry. Hence, we cannot and do not want to rely on any one method. Sometimes I work in a context where we are staring at 1,500 years of a performance tradition like Koodiyattam or Noh. Sometimes in a context where the most incredible thing in the theatre has happened last month. Theatre like this needs time to make. Engagements have to be at least two to three years long and only through repeated iterations of finding universals and specifics do we arrive at a theatrical language.

This sometimes succeeds and sometimes it is only a stepping stone for someone else to come and create the next step. In my view, the era in which we had grand masters who created a system of rehearsal which lasted for decades, production after production, is over. In all fields of work, we are heading to a world where there are no stable systems of ideology and culture that emerged after decolonization of the world. The initial excitement of finding the 'national' and making it synonymous to 'tradition' is over. By now, the world has understood hopefully that tradition and culture are more complex than nationalist identities. It is of little surprise that politically we see such a rise of right wing around the world because world over, politicians are feeling that globalization, if unchecked by narrow nationalism, will take away their claims to be true representatives of the people by ethnic exclusivity. Artists as always will move in the opposite direction. Hence, we see there is a continuous attempt in art to break the premise of singular identity being the identifier of the artwork.

We know that there are so many varied influences and motivations in a place in any culture that its stories need to dig deep into those, every time.

My collaborators, venues and audiences are constantly shifting. In fact, I came into the theatre for this freedom. To make work that is this varied. What is needed is to find a dramatic language every single time. For that our rooms need to be completely cued into the context, the music and the politics of that dramatic language which is being created in the rehearsal room we are in. To make work that moves through many borders, it is essential to understand the importance of specificity. To be form-diverse and structure-agnostic. To be able to read in more than one system.

Something that was first pointed out to me by my mother while I was at home.

3

The enterprise

I

The theatre is an ecology in itself. To produce, create, witness and admire a piece of theatre, a society needs several resources. People, money, objects, buildings and multiple opportunities to engage with good art are just some of the ingredients of a thriving theatre culture. Every community of theatre-makers and audiences needs active nurturing in order to ensure that it can respond to the needs of its time and also sustains a healthy art practice.

The Covid-19 pandemic time has led to the development of so much online theatre content, because theatre people are acutely aware of the need to create alternate ecologies for their work. An art form that takes pride in essentially being live pivoted so quickly to the recorded and hybrid mediums because theatre-makers are used to adapting. It is part of our job to keep finding ways of engaging with society. The medium is open to allow for constant change. In fact, that is its nature. The long-standing joke in the theatre world is that theatre has been a *dying* art for more than three thousand years.

Many people at different points of time have claimed that it will perish, but it has found a way of metamorphosing into something else. Plagues, fire, wars and large-scale migrations have altered theatre-making tools, techniques and enterprises since long. There is, in fact, some truth in saying that it is not the theatre but theatre enterprises that have indeed been dying and being reborn for three thousand years.

With time, space and context, theatre ecologies change. This leads to a change in the theatre enterprises and that ultimately determines the theatre of a particular place at that time. Hence, it is extremely important to evaluate the effectiveness of a theatre experience in its context and based on its intentions. Theatre-makers who make work in different kinds of theatre must be acutely aware of the different theatre ecologies they are working in. I believe the time when a director took their brand of theatre everywhere is over. Truly internationalist and diverse theatre has to evolve in a way that directors need to make theatre by understanding the context of work and not by bringing their predetermined style into different theatres. Every theatre ecology builds enterprises that uniquely serve its purpose. A theatre-maker who will be making work in the years to come will be required to be tuned in to these specific needs. The theatre-maker will need to bring their talent, vision and hard work to new spaces, but will have to leave at the door their ideas of what is good theatre in their own context.

II

The first plays I saw in my life were all produced by a community. It was also by and large around specific cultural festivals. Durga Pujo, a Bengali festival held every year between October and November for about five to seven days, was in my childhood a sustained introduction to great art. Every evening, our neighbouring Durga Pujo gatherings hosted some of the greatest theatre performances, dance recitals and concerts by great Indian masters. I was introduced to the Marxist theatre of Utpal Dutt, the feminist work of Mahasweta Devi that champions the subaltern, the textual genius of Shambhu Mitra, the urban feminism of Ashapurna Devi, the classical music of Ajoy Chakrabarty, to the depth of Bengali folk music in *Baul* and the mesmerizing dance of Kelucharan Mohapatra in the pandals of this festival. They were artists at the peak of their powers performing for a large and diverse audience. These performances had no tickets and were paid for by the money raised by the Durga Pujo committee. Patrons paid for the festival, and it was considered a success only if many people from diverse backgrounds came to see these shows. At night, we saw our first Satyajit Ray, Mrinal Sen, Ritwik Ghatak, De Sica, Fellini and Bergman on a big screen in an open ground. We would all go back home early morning and sleep through the day. Year after year this festival enriched our lives. The curation and diversity of the enterprise were not part of a conscious programme to run an arts centre. There were no brochures or board meetings. They were simply part of the culture.

The story goes that during the British rule when congregations were banned for non-religious purposes, Indians invented several religious occasions in order to meet and plan revolutionary activities. For this reason, this festival could only be celebrated outdoors and not inside people's houses. This peculiar reason has led to the growth and normalization of this culture. There are alternate stories as to how the festival started, but this is a prevalent one and it also suits what really happens culturally during the days of the festival.

The key point I am trying to make is that while working in different ecologies, it is important to understand how a culture has developed and arrived at where it has. At the heart of it, theatre-making is for a community, and once we know what are the underlying reasons for a community to engage with theatre or art in general, we are in a much better place to make work for it.

Theatre artists world over not only work for their own growth but inevitably for the culture and community they make work in. Art works by aggregation. A society that values great poetry is very likely to create conditions for great theatre. Hence, an artist must work at developing multiple facets of their culture. There is no competition in art. The more art there is, the better it is for artists and audiences. Unlike industries where finite resources are being used to create products to be sold to a finite market, art is about infinite resources and infinite mind-space. In multiple theatre cultures of the world, artists create enterprises which feed the contexts that essentially serve the community.

The notion of a modern industry that operates within competition and which exists uniquely for commercial reasons is an extremely new and localized idea in the history of theatre in many parts of the world. The commercialization and corporatization of theatre have created not only economies of scale but also several false barriers to entry. Directors and writers are known by their super-specializations from a very early age in such commercial theatre industries. Theatre-makers write on their resumes whether they work on classics or on new work. They have to mention their drama school and their interest in physical or textual theatre. However, these are all completely false barriers and markers borrowed from product industries. A contemporary theatre-maker's resume might be indicative of what they will not be making next. It is hardly indicative of what they would like to go on making. No self-respecting artist would want to commit to the future of their art based on their past achievements.

World over, theatre directors have created enterprises that allow them to grow their roots and branches. These enterprises help them forge their own way without compromising to the vision of the prevailing art market. If anything, their enterprises are like laboratories which change the reality of what their field understands today.

Young theatre artists who are starting out their practice often ask how and where do they get their work produced. Where do they begin? This is a universal question.

The answer is really simple. Make work in your community.

It can be in any space. On a terrace, under a tree, in a school building, by the side of the street. Absolutely anywhere that your community gathers. Make a livelihood from it if you can, and if not, do not impose that enormous responsibility on your art for some time. Work in a restaurant, teach extra classes, get a bicycle and do deliveries but make work. Create art that means something to you and your community. And create art every day. Give yourself some hours in which you will either make art alone or do it with friends who are in the same predicament. Stay together. This is when you are really learning how to make theatre. This is the real thing. Everything else afterwards in your career is a version of this. If you can make a performance with your friends that has meaning for your community with the resources in your houses, you can make theatre anywhere in the world. Every community holds all the complexities that any other does. Every community has questions, secrets, desires, taboos, love and violence. If you can stir these with your work, you are ready to make anything anywhere. Everything else is detail. Form that can be learnt, budgets that can be managed, teams that can be built and projects that can be delivered. There is no boundary to human learning and hence, no boundary to what might interest a theatre-maker. The possibility of reaching out for an infinity of ideas and meeting different cultures is exactly what makes the theatre such a delightful and fulfilling profession.

To get started, start in your neighbourhood. Make meaning for those you know, rest will follow. Remember always that not only are you working for the theatre, the theatre is also working for you. Behind your back. Your community is your marketing, finance and

HR team. They are your best agents and greatest PR company you can ever have. Be careful not to please them but to add meaning to their lives. Create art which as they say 'heals the scarred and provokes the comfortable'. Be that ripple in society that forces it to question itself. Communities can smell dishonesty and flattery from a mile. Do your job. Be an artist. Every day. That's it. Doesn't matter in how big a theatre or how well known a place. Doesn't matter how many people are in the audience or which reviewer is in the front row. Find your function in your community and serve that function. Everything else will happen.

III

When Sandeep Shikhar and I started Indian Ensemble, we were both unemployed, married and had multiple college degrees between us. He had studied economics in university and then completed a two-year degree programme in acting. After this, for almost a decade, he had been writing for television in Mumbai. He had come to Bangalore after getting married. He wanted to do something other than be in the rat race of the television industry.

I had studied physics and mathematics in university. This was followed by a stint in rural management, a management degree specializing in finance and then a two-year Lecoq-based degree programme at the London International School of Performing Arts (LISPA). I had come back to India because I did not want to work in the theatre *industry* in London and also because I found its monolingual nature limiting for my work.

I was twenty-nine, and he was thirty-two. We wanted to start our own company which made the work that we wanted to and the way we wanted to. We had both opted out of working in more organized industries and had a dream of recreating the experience of the culture and community we had been part of while growing up.

Indian Ensemble was formed on three principles:

1. We would always foreground the creative work. We would never take up any project for any other reason than a purely creative one. And we would make work with no compromise on time, effort and process even if we had to compromise financially.

2. All our training programmes would be free of cost. We had both studied on scholarships in theatre schools and were aware that many people would not be able to pursue a life in the theatre if the training itself cost money. It was also a way of removing this critical barrier to diversity in our programmes.
3. The income of the group would be shared equally by all members. Since we were all subsidizing the work through our time, all earnings of the company would be split in a given production among everyone irrespective of their role.

We developed three verticals in the company:

1. A theatre producing wing.
2. A theatre training wing, which by the end of our ten years had offered devising, playwriting and directing courses.
3. A social outreach programme that would reach out to our community in Bangalore and try to bring in a diverse audience into the theatre.

All Indian Ensemble shows were free for anyone who could not afford the tickets on first come, first serve basis. This added people from all walks of life to our audiences.

We had no money when we started. I worked in a school as a theatre teacher and Sandeep wrote some scripts remotely for television once in a while. I invested into our company much of what I earned from the school and some of the savings from money I was earning from doing some institutional workshops in India. People gave us rooms in schools and colleges for rehearsals. We were broke but we had the entire day to read, write and rehearse. My wife too invested her savings from a previous job she had in order to produce some of the work. She too had quit her job at this time and was attending a painting school. We were all running our houses on the minimum but were very excited, for we sensed that this was our opportunity to make our own work and lead our creative lives on our own terms.

In our first performance of a play called *Treadmill* (written by Sandeep and directed by me) there were five people on stage, four backstage and three people in the audience!

But we were sure of what we were trying. We were enjoying this work, and we knew that overall the company had meaning for the city we were in.

Over time, our plays started becoming extremely successful. *Treadmill* ran to many houseful shows for over five years. Other plays were made. They often ran quite successfully nationally and internationally for years. There were also multiple translations of our plays and the company started to be invited to prestigious theatre festivals and won several awards. We received national and international commissions. People started to come up to us and offered us financial assistance for our work.

All of this was never easy. We worked extremely hard to make these things happen, but our three guiding principles never changed. We never foregrounded any other reason than the creative, we never charged anyone for a training programme and we tried our best to reach out to people from diverse backgrounds and get them to the theatre.

After ten years of running Indian Ensemble, our associate director took over as artistic director and we moved on.

Whatever we have been able to do in our theatre lives is because of this company. It made us actors, directors, writers, producers and teachers. This was only possible because our model was suited for our temperament and the needs of our community. During our larger commissions, we were able to pay people significantly and often much more than a commercial company of our size. We were a small company with a large output. No one was paid salaries but everyone was always paid and paid equally. Our rehearsals were open and many youngsters would sit in our rehearsal just the way we had been allowed to by other directors in our younger days.

Irrespective of all the success, we knew that what we had earned most significantly was the goodwill of people. Our community in our city trusted us. Our audiences had faith in our practices. No matter how frequently we travelled and how many major festivals we performed in, we made sure we were relevant to the growth of the theatre community in Bangalore. Several writers and directors who are making new work today in India are ex-students of Indian Ensemble's training programmes. We also did not have any major publicity for us. Most of the commissions we had and most of our audiences came through word of mouth. We always believed that there was no better way to bring audiences and funders, and we waited for people to hear about us. There was never a hurry in the company to be known. There was to make work though.

We did not always succeed. We failed sometimes at finding the money and had to push the work by a few months. We created some plays that did not work at all. Some close friends and collaborators had to leave because of the long hours of commitment to the company without the guarantee of a salary. Sandeep and I were also privileged that we could stay afloat by whatever we earned outside of the company. We lived modestly but our demands from our life were being met in the theatre.

This company was formed on the lines of the Durga Pujo that we both had grown up seeing. Its goal was to bring the best possible art to the most people without having to rely on profits. The company, however, ended up making reasonable profits over time. All profits were shared equally.

I firmly believe that this extremely important part of our lives took shape because the company connected its day-to-day work with the community.

Every theatre-maker has an inner image of how they got into the theatre. It could be a school teacher who brought us to stage, a family member, a dinner ritual or a religious function. Whatever that image is, in my view, it holds the key to where and how one's theatre practice can begin and find its roots in. This inner image can see a person through many ups and downs of making theatre. Even now when I am flustered by anything anywhere in the world, I tell myself I can always go back to my Durga Pujo pandal and make whatever play I want. I know that I will have made a difference in my life and others.

I can always ask Sandeep and Ira (Irawati Karnik, writer, actor, old friend and frequent collaborator) to come into the room. If everything else fails we will still end up making theatre which matters to us and our community.

It is very reassuring.

IV

Jocelyn Clarke, my dear friend and dramaturg, has worked with several leading theatre-makers and institutions around the world. He has great insight about plays, processes and institutions.

Some years ago, we were together in Abu Dhabi and were discussing the future of Indian Ensemble. I felt at that time that we were at an important crossroad. A few years into running a company, an artistic director can get tired or muddled, or both!

One is continuously trying to think about the path ahead and, at the same time, is also dealing with the limitations of the work that has been done so far. After much ideation about the future, Jocelyn said to me, 'Your company is not what you think it is. It is what it does.' We sat and looked at our last three years of programming, and it was absolutely clear what the company was trying to become.

It was yearning for avenues to get new directors and smaller projects. To return in a sense to what it had started as. Over time, every project in Indian Ensemble had become high stakes and big budget. We had got trapped in our own success.

This led us to starting the Indian Ensemble Studio, which became a platform to create work in alternate spaces and lower budgets with younger directors. One of these directors, Chanakya Vyas, went on to become an associate director and then took over as artistic director of Indian Ensemble when we left. He led the company into many new directions, creating much more participatory and technology-driven work than in our time. The three principles were the only non-negotiables we passed on to him.

Around the world, there is a hegemony of the West End and the Broadway model of making theatre. Like most other hegemonic ideas from the West, a financially viable theatre enterprise often means a replica of these models. Especially outside of the United States and the United Kingdom, there is a way in which people are made to look up at these theatre ecologies as *the* models of success. It's a pity that most theatre cultures do not think about the German model as the gold standard, thereby pressurizing their governments to invest more in the arts. Instead, better process and professionalization are management buzzwords that are eating away at the best practices and processes of theatre cultures in non-industrial places.

No model is perfect. There are several problems with traditional models of Eastern dramatic forms. However, the solutions need to be found within a context. I am also aware that when I say 'the West', I do great disservice to the millions of ways in which the theatre of the Western world is extremely diverse, beyond the commercialization of West End or Broadway. It is all about nuance and context no matter where one is. It is extremely important for theatre-makers to not blindly emulate hegemonic ideas of theatre production.

Every theatre enterprise is a living thing. It is born in a context. It learns from the world as it grows, but it also keeps shaping its own context. Then it changes itself because the context has shifted slightly because of it. This constant dance, of the life of the enterprise and the culture it is in, is a vital part of theatre-making. These two aspects are inextricably linked.

I learnt at home a fundamental thing about the arts. That common people like us can love great art. Content that is meaningful, rich with metaphors and layering does not need audiences to be rich, highly educated or to be housed in an elite room with expensive upholstery. It is not a problem if there is opulence, but there is no inherent creative or intellectual connection between art and opulence.

A lot of lazy programming in the world is passed off on the myth that complex art is elitist. That common people are looking for art to escape the drudgery of their day-to-day life. This is the incorrigible nonsense that lazy producers use as an excuse to not travel, read and look. They pass on the failings of their responsibility to the audience. They believe common people are not smart and pass this thought as being a democratic and non-elitist idea.

Complex art needs work. It needs a thriving questioning culture and its art-makers need to trust human endeavour and ambition. Almost every theatre-maker in the history of theatre has created their best work by creating a shell that contains more than themselves. And this shell needs to keep expanding and including more and more common people.

I learnt at home that great art must have the possibility of failing among ordinary people. That ultimately the sign of a rich culture is that its poorest person can enjoy a Ray film or a Picasso painting. This is the only way a culture can create the next Ray or Picasso. My home taught me that art is contagious and one needs institutions to get people infected.

If the art is any good, it must work for its depth and not its novelty. Art that has depth can be attempted with less or more resources. It is the context, and not the budget, which matters in the end.

V

Our classes in NYU Abu Dhabi are extremely diverse. The students come from many different countries. Once while we were studying institutional dramaturgy, I asked my students to imagine that they were heads of a theatre and had to create a programme for a year. They could curate anything they wanted as if they had no restrictions of money or resources. The students had to make their submissions in a week.

In this first iteration, I noticed that all submissions were extremely close to each other. They had all been to a study-away programme in New York and the ideas of what they thought was good art were extremely similar and close to each other.

The following week we detailed the assignment. I asked them to answer the following questions and then create the annual programme again.

1. Where is your theatre? Which city, town or village?
2. Which community lives here? What are the most important conversations in this community? What would you like to develop in this community? What would you like to bring into this community and why?
3. Which processes of theatre-making are valuable here? Is this a culture of poetry, painting, books, ritual performances or any other form? Which is the go-to form in this culture for important conversations and entertainment?
4. How much work would you like them to see and is there work you would like them to participate in?
5. What will determine at the end of the year if your programme was successful or not?

This time after a week we had completely different submissions.

We had the vision of a travelling theatre company in Chile, which primarily performed for women. The vision of a large theatre in Gaza as a cultural centre, which tells stories that are not of the conflict. We had a large music hall in Harlem that was to push the boundaries of what is called 'Black music' and an alternate arts centre in Pakistan for producing queer work.

They had all arrived at the beginning of what is *their* theatre.

Part II

Away

4

Brecht in Kashmir

*The city from where no news can come,
Is now so visible in its curfewed nights
That the worst
Is precise.*

(AGHA SHAHID ALI)

Winter. Srinagar. Kashmir. 2008.

Another curfewed night had passed. Another night in which deathly silence was often interrupted by gunshots. In a city where by way of introduction within the few days I had been here, I had found myself walking along a street one moment and, in the next, realized for the first time in my life that an army sniper's gun was following my walk. I had stopped and waved at him. He had relaxed, waved back and asked me to move on. I did.

It was, however, morning now. One of those beautiful Srinagar mornings when the mountains shine. The Dal Lake in the heart of the city revealed two reflections moving towards each other since ages: one of the Islamic shrine of Hazratbal on the north, and to the south the Shankaracharya Temple of the Hindus.

Srinagar. If one were to click only its landscapes, one would indeed find a 'paradise on earth', as the great poet Amir Khusrau described it in the thirteenth century. However, the portraits of its people would reveal the scarred and shattered city that the other great poet, Agha Shahid Ali, wrote about in the twentieth century.

The curfew had opened up for a few hours, and I was drinking tea at a small tea shop close to the lake. My cramped broken-down guest house, watched over by a solitary guard with a machine gun, was right next door. The night had been freezing cold. The morning brought with it little sunlight and some hours of ease in the curfew. Together, this had brought people out on the streets after quite a few days of having to stay indoors.

The tea shop I was standing at was owned by a man armed with an extraordinary sense of humour and five tea glasses. He reasoned it was so cold that he could wash only as many cups at a time. If there was any sixth customer, and there always was, he had to wait.

This tea seller met people with the greatest of wits in the worst of times. Just two evenings ago, when I was there at his shop, an armed convoy of Jammu and Kashmir Police stopped before his shop, and the commanding officer rushed in with some of his soldiers for tea. Since the tea seller had only five cups, the soldiers had to wait for their turns. The impatient officer told him to hurry up since they were heading to an urgent mission. To which the tea seller calmly replied in Hindi, 'Sir, aapko jaldi hoti to chai peene thodi rukte?' (Sir, if you were in a real hurry, would you have stopped for tea?')

He often said he wanted *aazadi*, or freedom. The word is a chant in Kashmir and heard on a daily basis, resonating loudly during protests against the Indian occupation of Kashmir. It is also written on walls, which the security forces paint over with slogans like 'Mera Bharat Mahaan' (My India Is Great). But the *aazadi* he spoke of was from making tea.

'I do not care if we stay with India, Pakistan or become free. But someone please liberate me from washing tea cups in the winter!'

I was standing there in a jacket, pyjamas and woollen socks donned over slippers. I was researching in Kashmir for something that might turn into a play. I had already directed and devised a play called *Rizwaan*, based on the poetry of the Kashmiri American poet, Agha Shahid Ali. Particularly his collection called *The Country Without a Post Office*. I was then part of Writer's Bloc, a playwright residency in India conducted by Rage Theatre (Mumbai), along with Royal Court Theatre's International Department with Elyse Dodgson at the helm. After the first part of the workshop, we were asked what we would want to write about, and I had found myself saying that this time I would like to go to Kashmir for research and find out if there is a play I could build from that. But I had no money to make that trip, and so, Rajit Kapur, the brilliant actor and one of the founders of Rage, stepped forward to fund it from his own pocket.

In Kashmir, I had been interviewing people through the day whenever there was no curfew. By 7.00 pm, I would be sitting at a coffee shop next to my guest house, the only place with heating. The interviews covered a range of people. From soldiers, journalists, students, doctors – including those in the government psychiatry hospital – to the leads I was getting of people outside Srinagar, in areas where the conflict between the armed forces and the armed resistance was heavy. Most of these interviews revolved around discussions on contemporary Kashmir. But I had not yet decided on any real focal point for what could become my play. Kashmir had innumerable stories and with every slight change of lens, an entire new way of looking at its conflict was revealing itself to me.

I would make notes and later chat with a man who ran the coffee shop with heating. On nights when there was no curfew, the shop would remain open as long as both of us wanted. There was hardly anyone else who ever came. He knew I was a writer and wanted me to write about Kashmir. When I had told him I write for theatre, he sceptically asked if it would be shown on television. Not at all, I told him. In fact, what I was doing would be live. He was still confused, and so, I explained this was more like Bhand Pather, a traditional folk theatre form of Kashmir.

'Okay', he smiled. 'I like *Bhand*.' (A word used to refer to the form of Bhand Pather, and that also means a clown.) 'I believe them although they make fun of everyone. Yes, I believe them. They tell the truth.'

The deal was sealed. I had made it in. He believed in the theatre and would keep the place open for me on non-curfew nights and also keep checking on my notes with great interest. He never commented on them immediately but at times, when he found something that he believed needed more clarity, he would bring it up in one or two days in a passing remark.

Several times in my life, when faced with adverse situations with authorities, mobs, security forces or others who have wanted to ban my plays or make me change what I am writing, I have gone back to this conversation and many others like it. Time and again, in some of the most occupied places on earth, I have found people sharing their entire lives with me at the risk of death. Housing me, feeding me, providing me a security cover on knowing I was about to write a play. I am not sure if other forms invite the same faith, but for some reason I have always found people believe in theatre. They have wondered if it is a real profession, and many times asked if it pays at all and if my family is happy with what I do. But the one thing that inadvertently exists is this incredible faith in the theatre. In hundreds of such encounters across the world, people have opened up to me knowing this was about making a play and somehow it meant to them the work would be uncompromising with the truth.

Coming back to the morning at the tea shop, I had just received my tea, and the market at Dalgate was bustling. The buses had started to ply and people were heading out from Srinagar to their villages and towns within this window between curfews.

I was standing at the entrance of the tiny shop with my glass of tea and a piece of Kashmiri bread in my hand. A young boy of about twenty came and stood next to me with his tea. I had just turned thirty, with a quick celebration at home at midnight just before leaving for Kashmir. We smiled at each other and he asked me abruptly, 'Are you Indian?'

I told him I was. I was new to Kashmir and was still getting used to the reality that Kashmiris do not think of themselves as Indians, in the same manner as Indians do not think of themselves as British. This went against what I had learnt in school, that Kashmir was an integral part of India, in the same way that up until the mid-twentieth century the British grew up thinking that the only significant thing about India was that it was the crown of their empire.

'How come you are here at this time?' he asked because this was not quite the tourist season.

'Just like that', I smilingly said. I was a bit sceptical of taking this conversation further because it was boys of his age who were throwing stones on Indian security forces. In fact, the curfew had been imposed because the stone-throwing had become unstoppable. These were not armed militia or freedom fighters with guns but young boys – sometimes girls – with black cloths covering their faces, facing machine guns and armoured vehicles in hundreds and thousands with just stones in their hands. They were aggressive, fearless and chanting for *aazadi*.

I was Indian, male, thirty. I embodied everything he had reason to hate.

I was terrified at the prospect that this boy could be one of the stone-throwers and was getting friendly with the intention of bringing me to some harm.

'Just like that? What do you do?'

I gathered some courage and told him I write.

'Write what?'

'Plays.'

'Plays?'

'Yes, plays.'

I was about to explain about Bhand Pather again when he said, 'Do you know Brecht?'

I was taken aback, to say the least. 'Yes, somewhat.'

'I love Brecht. We all do. He is a Kashmiri writer. He writes for us. Can you write like him?'

I was astonished by his question. 'No,' I truthfully answered.

'I am sorry.' I laughed now. 'I do not write like Brecht as much as I would love to.'

'Will you be my friend? I do not have an Indian friend.'

'Yes. Of course.'

'Then come with me. I'll take you to my teacher's house.'

At this moment, I was very worried, wondering how safe would it be. What if he were to take me somewhere and . . .?

He was not going to kill me, was he? Were his friends going to lynch me to death?

However, this had never happened in Kashmir. No civilian Indian in Kashmir had ever been killed by its people to my knowledge. In fact, if anything, even in my short stay, the people had been extraordinarily nice to me. Over and over again, whenever the aspect of writing a play came up, they had been very open and poured out their lives.

In an extremely selfish manner, I caught myself thinking that I had come here for research and here was research walking up to me. Why would I say no to it? I had come to Kashmir to understand, to ask questions, to listen – and here he was, and I hadn't even asked his name.

'Faizan,' he told me. 'Yourself?'

'Abhishek.'

'So, shall we go now?'

'Now?' I asked.

'Yes, let's go. What if suddenly there is a curfew again? Or a shoot-out? Or something else? How will we meet then?'

In Kashmir, this is a real thing. People often tell each other by way of leaving, 'If we are alive, we shall meet again.'
'Yes,' I said.

And so, we were on a bus to his teacher's house, who held classes at home for students in the neighbourhood since schools and colleges had been shut for a while.

The bus went around the beautiful Dal Lake towards Hyderpora on the other side of Lal Chowk, the centre of town where many flare-ups erupt between the protestors and the armed forces.

We had to stand on its steps for some time before managing to squeeze inside as it was full of people who had desperately come to the market around the lake to buy essentials.

In Kashmir, often there were two curfews. One imposed by the army and then the other ordered in protest by Hurriyat Conference, a major political party in Kashmir that had demanded complete independence from India. All work had to happen in between these two curfews; the people constantly manoeuvring their lives around them. Eventually, the play I wrote, *Djinns of Eidgah*, had a plot-line revolving considerably around these two curfews and how young people have to negotiate them. In the play, Bilal, a young football player, is up for trials to get selected for a club in Brazil and at one point has to sneak in to a morgue to take shoes off a dead person's feet since he cannot repair his own before the trials due to the curfews.

On the way, Faizan kept showing me different localities from the window. He pointed to a place and explained its significance in the life of the protests in Kashmir, informing me in which areas were the boys dominating and in which area the presence of CRPF (Central Reserved Police Force, a paramilitary force of the Indian state) was stronger. He was studying literature in Kashmir University.

'What classes are you taking?'
He opened his bag and showed me.
There were two articles in his bag.

A stone. And a collection titled *Western Drama*, or something like that which I do not remember clearly now.

I asked him again what he was studying and he took on the demeanour of an actor. His face changed, body firmed up as if preparing for a performance and he looked me straight in the eyes and with some affection said –

'When the houses of the great collapse,
Many little people are slain.'

He smiled, 'Brecht, my friend. Brecht.'

Before I could say anything, or even begin to understand the experience I was in the middle of, he pointed to a row of houses through the window and said, 'These are the houses of the slain.'

Although he was still a student and much younger to me, Faizan is one of the greatest English-language teachers I have met. He spoke in completely broken English, and yet could aptly quote Brecht in context, which he amply did in the days to come. Growing up in India, like in any post-colonial context, we were trained to feel inferior when we did not know the master's language. Even today in most parts of India, being able to speak good English is not only practically and financially very useful, it is also a marker of social status and acceptance. However, in my view, students in Kashmir do not have the same post-colonial anxieties as Indians. Perhaps, being twice colonized, they have a completely different relationship to the language of their former master. To them, it is potentially a language of liberation when one can quote and speak in the language the present master was oppressed with.

We reached Hyderpora and got down from the bus. We walked some lanes, crossing the backs of houses and Faizan opened a large gate of a massive house. As we walked in, I saw a large pile of rocks next to the gate.

Faizan opened his bag and chucked the stone right into the pile. 'After class, we will go to throw them.'

I was already beginning to think about his deep conviction in Brecht and in throwing stones. Every day, he went with many boys his age and faced tear gas and bullets with just stones in their hands. But were they all also armed with something quite invisible to the state?

Were they armed with Brecht, Agha Shahid, Shakespeare and Marlowe?

Was it this that the Indian state was unable to see? In fact, wasn't this invisible presence exactly what several writers, poets and students under oppressive regimes were imprisoned and tortured for?

Wasn't Orhan Kemal sent to jail in Turkey when he was around the same age as Faizan? Wasn't he imprisoned solely because he was reading Maxim Gorky and Nâzım Hikmet? Wasn't Kemal reading exactly the way Faizan read Brecht? By reading literature while looking at his own surroundings for context.

It seemed to me that the fundamental threat of literature had remained unchanged, although the regimes themselves had changed in nature. Had in fact gotten much more powerful over time. However, ironically, it was also in prison that Orhan Kemal got to share his cell with his literary hero, the poet Nâzım Hikmet, himself. Instead of destroying the intellectual and creative possibilities of Orhan Kemal, the regime had essentially handed him the greatest literature school in the world. Several months of Nâzım Hikmet's attention, and the tutelage of classics under him, led Kemal to become the writer he became: the voice of the poor in Turkey with an unrelenting scrutiny of power. Clearly, the regime had no idea that ideas of freedom and literature unstoppably diffuse into each other like osmosis.

Faizan and his friends were being armed in the same way by their teacher. They were not being trained to shoot, aim, steal or run. They were being trained in drama and poetry. The real difference between a soldier and a revolutionary is not in the ammunition. The difference is in the metaphor.

It is the metaphor of life that drives people to be fearless in the face of death. A flag and a play are fundamentally at odds with each other. One is a symbol and the other a nuance. This, in my view, is the reason why regimes are so opposed to literature and drama. Nuance is ultimately the greatest enemy of nationalism.

As I think today about the walk up to that room full of young Kashmiri students, I cannot help but think about the moment before a play begins. The anticipation that anything might happen and, on certain days, the strong feeling that whatever happens next will change my life forever. Theatre has given me several of these moments. Sometimes in rehearsals, sometimes as an audience, and very often while working on the play during its research.

I am often asked, how does the research translate to scenes? To answer truthfully, research in arts practice is about memory and imprint rather than the thesis. I value thesis, of course. The thesis that is formed not only after research but during the multi-layered process of writing and rehearsing, and that forms the choices of the play to a large extent. But the theatre that presents this thesis – the images, the sounds, the characters – is a matter of impression.

We go to theatre with a paradoxical ambition: of wanting to remember the future. We want to know what happens next, where we are headed, but at the same time we want to remember our childhood, parents, ancestors and the beginning of the cosmos. This is intrinsic to the act of making theatre.

When I think of walking up to Faizan's makeshift classroom in his teacher's house, I am left with a gap in my memory. I can remember the feeling, but I cannot remember if I heard the young boys and girls first and then felt something was about to change my life, or if I felt that way first and then the door opened to reveal the students.

A room full of young Kashmiri boys and girls, most of them in late school and early university – bright, raring to change the world, as optimistic as any other congregation in the world, as aspirational, as vulnerable, as anarchic and as full of possibilities – had gathered here for this class.

But what class was this? Was this part of a curriculum? If so, which one? Which class and what level?

But they did not seem to belong to the same age group entirely. This was not a regular class: they were here to learn, and that's it. Just purely to learn and to read, and then later, to go out and throw stones at the armed forces.

This teacher had surely taught them all at some time. In high school, perhaps. And they were all back because he still had something to offer. I had heard of another professor in Kashmir University whom I met later: professor Hameeda Nayeem, whose classes on poetry and drama would be packed with students. A few years later, I went to Kashmir University for a seminar on Agha Shahid Ali that was organized by her and I could feel the charge in the room. There was a reading of some scenes of *Rizwaan*, among other things. As a playwright, I had heard that play read and performed in several languages, but in that room in Kashmir, it suddenly became a living document. When the young girls read with quivering voices the scene where Rizwaan meets his sister after dying, I could tell that they knew the relationship between life, war and theatre. Directly.

However, that was later. I am thinking about it now as I am thinking about climbing the steps of the teacher's house and opening the door. Two incidents which are both in the past are emerging at this point of time in that order, I think, because thinking about theatre is essentially thinking about a collage of memory ordered by feeling.

I am thinking of the two incidents as the same incident because they felt the same.

The two rooms. Led by two teachers and charged by their students.

I entered the room and saw they were indeed reading Brecht. Discussing lines of text, context and casting each other to perform small sections. They also had a Kashmiri translation of a Brecht play, though I cannot recall which one. They were getting ready to do some bits in the class when we entered and everyone went quiet.

I greeted the teacher and the students, and they greeted me back. With a smile. Faizan explained to the teacher and the class who I was. They were absolutely delighted that I made plays.

I should point out here that this was a huge leap of faith for them. I could have been from the police or an agent of the government of India, and there are many of those. The coincidence of a playwright meeting a revolutionary who loved Brecht that morning at the tea shop was quite exceptional. They did not know if I had started speaking to Faizan and then made up the story of my interest in his class or if he had invited a theatre-maker after running into me by chance.

Their teacher approached me and welcomed me in to his class, asking me to sit down. He asked if I wanted some *noon-chai*, the salted tea which Kashmiris usually drink, or Lipton *chai*, which could be any regular tea bag dipped in hot water, not necessarily Lipton. I politely replied I did not want to bother the class and he politely refused to not oblige. Soon, I was sitting with a cup of Lipton *chai*, and we were all talking of Kashmir and its stories.

I learnt about a performer in Budgam, who was killed by the armed forces because he refused to give them part of his costume. He had dressed as a clown – I guessed he was playing a *bhand* (clown) from Bhand Pather, but I could be wrong; it could have also been a contemporary play – and a few soldiers of a nearby barrack had surrounded him when he was returning home. Apparently, they had seen his performance and loved it.

They wanted to have some pictures clicked with him, to which he gladly obliged. He turned to walk back with his brother when the soldiers asked him to give them a part of his costume. The two brothers refused and got into a brawl with the soldiers. The soldiers outnumbered them and they were badly beaten up. After a few days, the clown succumbed to his injuries. The brother later spoke of how in the performance they were coming from, his brother had lines which meant 'I can never be killed'.

Several years later, I came to know of a play in Damascus in which an actor was performing as Gilgamesh, the one who cannot die. While the performance was going on, the theatre was bombed. As people started running out, they saw the actor playing Gilgamesh lying dead on the floor – and stopped for a moment. They had believed for the last hour or so, there in that theatre with all their heart, that Gilgamesh cannot die. And now the impossible had happened: he was dead before their eyes. For a moment, I was told, the shock of how theatre could have lied to them was greater than that of the theatre being bombed.

A young boy in the classroom said that sometimes on India's Independence Day or Republic Day, the Indian armed forces would ask youngsters to perform plays in schools and local gatherings. 'We do not use any characters with colourful costume. They might want it later.'

About seven years later, *Djinns of Eidgah* was translated to Kashmiri by a great stalwart of Kashmiri theatre, Bhavani Bashir. I went to his theatre space, Ensemble Kashmiri Theatre Akademi (EKTA) in Srinagar, and the place had been ravaged by the horrific floods of the Jhelum River that flows through Srinagar. Bhavani *Sahab* showed me around his theatre building and took me particularly to the costume-room where he showed me the wide range of costumes their company had. 'We really worked hard to protect this', he told me. 'Nowadays, it is hard to make these clothes.'

'Why?' I asked.

'Who will make them anymore? Many craftsmen have left and several others have died.'

The costume rack of a theatre group can often reveal significantly about the politics of the place. The more colonized the region, the stronger the theatre community of that place fights to preserve the diversity of its costumes. In a land of soldiers and uniforms, the costume shop is a site of rebellion through cloth.

In Faizan's class, the free-flowing conversation went from individual lives to stories of those who had been martyred while protesting. We spoke about ideas, lines of text and then there were small performances of scenes.

I was watching them enact scenes from their favourite Brecht plays, and it was extraordinary to see what was worthy of a laugh and what wasn't in this room. Jokes on the powerful were clearly high on receiving laughs but scenes where common people get beaten up, even in a comic manner, were not comic. For they had been beaten themselves. They knew its reality. They knew there were men in their houses who had been electrocuted in the penis so they could no longer have children, and there were women who had been raped. They did not find torture of the powerless Black comedy. The genre had lost its significance.

They asked me for notes since I was a professional, and I told them I was in no position to comment. That in my theatre, we need years of training and use innumerable methods to achieve the nuance they had already brought to their scenes.

They asked me if I would come with them to throw stones. I said yes but I would not throw any. I would like to be with them to see what it was like, if they did not mind.

They were more than happy and promised me that if I were to write their story, they would form a circle around me, so that in case the forces started firing, I would not be hit. I told them that would not be required. If I was with them, I was with them like them. They would not need to do anything extra to protect me.

Many of the people and places that became part of my research later were leads from this encounter with Faizan, his teacher and friends. In the days to come, I saw the stone-throwing from both vantages. With those who threw the stones and also from a CRPF bunker, watching hundreds of boys – and a significant number of girls – approach us with stones. It was undoubtedly educative to be on both sides and to try to understand what it feels like on either side. The CRPF soldiers too had agreed to let me stay with them because they somehow intrinsically believed in the act of theatre. They had not seen many plays but I suppose in many cultures, like in India, one encounters theatre from childhood through ritual and with family. It is not considered to be a profession necessarily but, in my view, people intrinsically assign a truth value to it. It stands for something uncompromised.

The time for curfew was approaching and so I got ready to leave. The teacher, accompanied by many students, came to the gate to see me off. Faizan told me he would drop me to the bus back to Dalgate.

At the bus stop, he asked me if I was really going to write about them. I said yes, I would.

'Look, we did not hurt you. You know we are not bad people.'

I emphatically agreed.

'The media is making us out to be terrorists. Do you think we are terrorists?'

'No.'

'In your play, will you cast me? If it happens in Delhi or Bombay, please give me a role that has a good costume.'

'Yes', I told him.

Faizan is now a father. His child is now in school. He has read *Djinns of Eidgah* and still asks me, 'So when will I act in your plays? What role will I get?'

I tell him no matter what role, he can choose his own costume.

He tells me Brecht brought us together.

I tell him you made me realize why theatre exists and why clowns die for their costumes.

I have been to Kashmir several times since then. It is almost my second home. I have had the great joy of interacting with theatre-makers of Kashmir, who create incredible work in extremely dire circumstances. They could of course be doing many other things. Theatre is by no means lucrative in Kashmir nor is it particularly safe to tell stories that critique power.

However, in my view, Kashmir and theatre from Kashmir are a model for the world. A gold standard and reassurance for anyone who has ever had doubts about why people make theatre.

Among other reasons, Kashmir has survived because of its storytellers. Dastan Goi, a form of Persian, Urdu and Kashmiri storytelling, used to play on Radio Kashmir until the early 1980s. But it was stopped by the Indian state because even if the state understood the words through translators, it still suspected that messages were being passed through these stories. Likewise, during the mutiny of 1857, the British banned the telling of several Indian folk tales because they suspected Indians were passing messages through these stories.

In a way, I think it is true. I do not think people of Kashmir actually pass details of anti-state activities through stories, but through them, they do pass on information crucial to life. That beyond the bright lights, tickets, glamour of any major theatre industry of the world, sometimes the reason to make theatre is to just survive with dignity in the midst of constant oppression. It is not what is called 'activist theatre' or 'theatre for development'. It is purely aesthetic. It is productions of *Hamlet*, *Macbeth*, *Caucasian Chalk Circle*, *Habba Khatoon*, *Alif Laila* and new works on real incidents.

In Kashmir, theatre is made because it is a form of memory. The memory involves the word, the gesture, the story, the space and even the costume.

All of which one has to claim from the state.
The theatre becomes a site of claiming.
A site of life where both meaning and spectacle can coexist.
A site of life amidst the normalization of death.

It is night.
The married couples
Lie in their beds. The young women
Will bear orphans.

(BRECHT)

5

The Kashmir trilogy

I

I am sure this happens to every storyteller. One has a story etched in their mind long before they ever imagined working on it. A story whose roots can only be roughly estimated in hindsight but for which there is no clear explanation.

I will never be able to clearly explain why Kashmir has always meant so much to me. Why, while I was a student in London, it was so clear to me that I'll come back to India and then go to Kashmir. I used to say this with the certainty of someone who belongs to Kashmir, and there is no explanation for it. Today, after so many years of association with Kashmir, when some of my work exists in Kashmiri and when Kashmir is almost my second home, I still cannot explain what drove me so automatically and compulsively to seek the first stop of my journey outside home in this beautiful and yet strife-torn valley in the mountains.

I imagine it has to do with the idea since my childhood that there was a continuous attempt by the media and the state to not tell us the complete truth about Kashmir. As if something *had* to be kept from us. Throughout my life, Kashmir has been in the news. Every single week there has been news of terrorist attacks, of armed conflict between soldiers and suspected militants or an armed engagement with Pakistan at the borders. I had some Kashmiri friends, most of them Kashmiri Hindus who had left Kashmir around 1989. The only Muslim man I knew from Kashmir was a shawl-seller who used to visit our house every summer. He used to be in Delhi in the summer and return home just before winters.

Then during my college years, the Kargil conflict erupted between India and Pakistan in the northern mountains of Kashmir. I started going to Old Delhi railway station every evening as a volunteer with a newspaper that distributed fancy food-packets from the Taj Hotels as a souvenir to soldiers who were going to fight the war in special trains. I overheard many of the interviews that were being conducted by the press at the station. Suddenly, I had faces and context to the people who were often referred to as a group or in numbers in the pages of the newspaper every morning. The stories swelled by the end of the conflict. Two of my seniors from college who were army officers died in the conflict. We used to play football together till some years ago, and this was the closest I had gotten to the conflict.

The cost of human life was enormous, and yet it felt like key parts of the story were being kept away from us. It was clear to me that this place between India, Pakistan and China had been in the news for twenty years with everyone claiming to resolve its conflicts on priority, but no one was even close to achieving that.

I can only speculate in hindsight that these were perhaps some of the reasons for my hunch to go to Kashmir and search for what were the many truths. Nonetheless, I strongly recommend anyone starting out as a theatre-maker to take their hunches seriously. These are images and instincts that are present in us much before we start engaging with the world as professional storytellers. Hence, these images and ideas are not always understandable to us the way later themes and more articulated interests are. However, chasing these hunches can become the bedrock of one's foundational art practice.

II

Rizwaan: The gate keeper of paradise

Agha Shahid Ali's collection of poetry *The Country Without a Post Office* arrived in my post, thanks to Jisha Menon. Jisha teaches performance studies at Stanford, and we had worked together on a play in Bangalore. She had sent this life-altering collection to me as a present.

Agha Shahid was a Kashmiri American poet who lived and worked between Chicago and Srinagar. Agha Shahid's poetry has images and music than can haunt one for life. His collections are replete with poems of different registers which unravel the story of Kashmir layer by layer.

I was particularly intrigued by the name Rizwaan, which appears more than once in the collection. *Rizwaan* in Urdu means 'the gatekeeper of paradise'.

In a poem titled 'I See Kashmir from Delhi at Midnight', Shahid writes about a dream in which Rizwaan is being tortured and killed in an interrogation. As a tyre burns and drips on his back, Rizwaan dies screaming, 'I know nothing . . . I know nothing.' He asks the poet to tell his father that he won't be able to return home.

In another poem towards the end, there is a description of how Rizwaan actually dies by bleeding on the snow. And the central page of the book is a letter that Agha Shahid received from a friend in which he is informed about Rizwaan's death. In a sense, Rizwaan dies thrice in the collection: in a dream, in a real event and then in the news of his death.

The book also in parallel chronicles the taking over of the Dal Lake, the heart of Srinagar by the Indian armed forces. The post offices that were on the lake in boats are lost to the conflict and no one receives letters anymore. The book receives its title from this metaphoric loss of existence.

In 2009, when I was invited by the Film and Television Institute of India (FTII) in Pune to direct a play with their acting students, I went with this collection. There was no play text and no plan other than to devise with the students from scratch. We had a month and the words of Agha Shahid Ali.

To start with, the students and I read the poems by ourselves.

This was followed by a central question that would drive our rehearsal. The question was, 'When does someone or something really cease to exist? Is it when we dream of its death or when we receive the news of its death, or when it actually happens?'

This led us to design a series of improvisations around this question. The actors chose characters from the book of poems, and we improvised scenes around the imagined lives of these characters. Their lives were to overlap with the birth, growing up and death of Rizwaan.

Four kinds of improvisations were explored as provocations in the rehearsal room:

1. In a group, create a scene from Rizwaan's life that tells us something important about his family and its struggle to survive in the valley due to the conflict.
2. In a group, find a way of staging any section of a poem from the collection. This could be done using any imaginative formal proposition such as use of dance, music, puppetry or anything else that is theatrical in nature.
3. In a group, create a movement sequence that elaborates our central question.
4. Individually, write down an incidence of loss in your life and try to identify the specifics of that feeling. Now, in a group, try to create a scene from Rizwaan's life that allows each one of you to create your sense of loss irrespective of the character you are playing. In these scenes, Rizwaan could be present physically or referred to.

We used to meet every morning at 7.00 am for physical exercises and to prepare for the physical language of the play. We worked on the basics of an Indian martial-art form called Kalarippayattu. We also worked on building stamina and physicalizing the Rasa theory by finding physical gestures for each of the nine rasas: *karuna* (compassion), *raudra* (anger), *adbhuta* (wonder), *shringara* (love), *hasya* (laughter), *bibhatsa* (disgust), *bhayanaka* (fear), *veera* (valour) and *shantam* (bliss or peace). After working on the physical conditioning sessions, we would part at about 8.15 am for shower and breakfast. At 9.00 am, we would be back in rehearsal.

We would often start right away with new improvisations. Post-lunch we would start to refine the improvisations to get closer to scene structures. After 6.00 pm, we would go back to our rooms, and from 7.00 pm to late night I would write the scenes. The next day we would be in rehearsal with drafts of written scenes to rehearse and new improvisations to work on. As we moved closer to the opening, our scenes started to get more fixed and stable and our approach shifted to being more about the nuance of the performances instead of generating new material.

We used Agha Shahid's poetry in English, and I wrote in both Urdu and English. The play opened on the main stage of the FTII. Unfortunately, we could do only two performances with the original cast as this was part of their coursework and the programme allowed only two performances. A film-direction student of the college made a half-hour film on Rizwaan as her final diploma project.

The play was revived by the Indian Ensemble in Bangalore a few months later with actors from the city. It also went to be rehearsed in French by the actors of the Théâtre du Soleil and was published in the French magazine *Théâtre/Public* in 2016. The improvisational method of devising was itself inspired by the methods of Ariane Mnouchkine, the legendary director of Théâtre du Soleil. It was truly a great moment for me to see this play about Kashmir written in Urdu with students from Pune using methods devised by a French director find a performance with actors of that director in Paris.

The play also had a month-long Bangla production in Dhaka. Bangladesh's legendary theatre director Jameel Ahmed staged this play in the month of Ramzan as a way of reflecting on Islam and people's struggles.

III

Djinns of Eidgah

Once Rizwaan had opened in 2010, I felt strongly that now I had to get to Kashmir. We had researched on the story of Rizwaan through interviews and books but I had never been to the valley. The closest I had gone was to Jammu, which is the Hindu-majority part of Jammu and Kashmir. I was continuing to read in much greater detail about the conflict but did not have the resources to go to Kashmir.

In 2010, I was selected for a writer's residency jointly run by Elyse Dodgson of Royal Court Theatre and Rage Theatre Mumbai. The workshop was residential and had two parts to it. The first part was a residency in which all of us writers participated in a series of exercises, and then we had to propose a play that we wanted to write. We had to go away for a few months and write a draft of our play. In the second part, we would work on the drafts. Finally, these plays would be part of a festival called the Writer's Bloc festival in Mumbai and all of them would be produced there.

Djinns of Eidgah had a really long journey. It eventually became part of the Royal Court International Writer's residency in 2011, and in 2014 was produced at the Jerwood Theatre Upstairs at the Royal Court. I am containing this part of the chapter to key reflections that might be useful for theatre-makers, students of theatre or audiences to get closer to what were the key elements of this process. I am not describing the writing process in detail as I am doing that for another play, *Pah-la*, in this book. Also, the chapter 'Brecht in Kashmir' contains the frame of the world of the play and its complexities, hopefully in some detail. Hence, here I am reflecting on the key ideas, tools and learnings.

Research

I could go to Kashmir, thanks to actor and co-founder of Rage Theatre, Rajit Kapur. He paid for my tickets. Else, I would not have been able to begin. It was early in my career, and it was very reassuring. Since then, I have heard such stories of support many times across countries and in the lives of almost all artists. One must acknowledge the role that established artists have played in the lives of those who are to make a start. To believe in another person's art is as important, if not more, than believing in one's own. The theatre is replete with such examples. I owe Rajit and people like him immensely.

Kashmir in many ways has taught me how to conduct research for a play. I went in with leads from friends who were journalists, social workers and doctors. From there, bit by bit, adding one link to another, I had to find all the people I needed to meet to have a sense of the place. And this happened over multiple trips and multiple conversations over a span of about five years. The play was drafted eleven times during this period.

There are several worlds inside the play. The world of the children involved in the stone-throwing against the armed forces, the world of the psychiatry hospital with both doctors and patients, the world of Indian soldiers posted in Kashmir and the world of the insurgent forces fighting against the Indian armed forces. The worlds of the play open up in work like this as one builds trust. Gradually. This involves working with compassion, working on one's listening and being available to take risks. Some of it can be planned and some of it are accidents that change the shape of the work.

We must remember as playwrights that creative writing of this kind is closer to cultural anthropology than working in history or journalism. The research must include the seemingly banal as much as it should focus on life-changing events. In fact, it is the creation of this inner picture of what people eat, feel and wear that takes years. The big things are easier. It is not too difficult to find out dates of crackdowns and attacks. The playwright's job is to find out what it means to leave a meal halfway and run during a shoot-out. What it means to discover that a child has PTSD because she can no longer differentiate between a shoot-out and an avalanche. What it means to cross the border between India and Pakistan at night unnoticed by armed forces and what it means to bury one's third child in a burial ground after he was shot dead by the armed forces at the funeral of his older brother. And these are not stories. Some of this needs to be experienced. Some of it is found out by nurturing relationships over a long period of time. I am not a big believer of method-acting, but I surely do believe in method-writing.

My golden rules for this kind of research are summed up in these seven tenets:

1. EAT with the family. Once you are at a place where you can eat a meal together with those you are talking to, a real conversation can happen. Food gives us both intimacy and time to think.

2. EXPERIENCE danger. If you are writing about a shoot-out, a police attack, meeting an insurgent or being inside a stone-pelting crowd of children, make sure you have been there. It is impossible to draw these experiences from one's usual life.

3. LISTEN over record. Do not use a tape recorder, phone or any other device to record the conversation as a person speaks. It is a completely unnatural thing to do. It changes the conversation completely. Listen deeply. There are only a few facts to a deep crisis in someone's life. The real detail is in how they remember it, what is the quality of the silence, how many times they have repeated something and how it makes you both feel together. Write it on returning to your

pad. Cross-check when in doubt. Do not record and reduce the relationship. Sharpen your listening and memory.
4. READ a vast syllabus before interviewing. This way interviews are richer and one is not asking for things which are already in the books.
5. TELL people with complete clarity what you are interviewing them for. I always tell them that I am writing a play. That I am not going to write something that is black or white. It is not to say that there are no black and whites in the world or that every story necessarily has two sides. Some kinds of oppression are absolute. Some evil is pure. Some love can be unconditional. But I tell them that is the kind of thing that generally does not find its way into my plays because I think for those extremes, one does not need the theatre. However, I am also interested in challenging the powerful through the theatre. That is my premise. My pitch for an interview. I think it is very important for a writer to make their own intent and method clear.
6. SEND drafts to the people you interview for them to read. If they feel uncomfortable with a portrayal because it seems too close to them or if they find something inaccurate, take it out. If they feel what you have inferred about the situation is fundamentally flawed, rethink, revise and re-present the draft. People who have lived these lives are obviously very perceptive about what is being said. About the grey areas. You owe correct representation to these people and to no one else.
7. SIGN UP for this work only if you are prepared for its physical, emotional and psychological toll. Writing about Kashmir is like life and death for me. So was it when I was writing on Tibet. I would not be able to do it for a world I did not feel so connected to no matter how intellectually compelling it could be to do so.

Metaphor

The djinns appeared in *Djinns of Eidgah* through a process of identifying a motif through the research. Several people spoke about the role of djinns in the understanding of Kashmir.

There were djinns that needed to be exorcized after Papa II (Indian Army's torture chamber) was shut down and the house was given to a bureaucrat. The house where Papa II was located on Gupkar Road in Srinagar is one of the most beautiful houses I have ever seen. It was a torture chamber, nightmares of which still wake people up at night. The first house on that road is the UN head office in Srinagar. The UN office has always known that the torture chamber was down the road.

There are djinns in Ali Masjid, the mosque next to the Eidgah, that is, the martyrs' graveyard. There are djinns that faith healers try to exorcise in those patients who are referred to them by psychiatrists. (In Kashmir, faith healers and psychiatrists refer people to each other. There is no contradiction.)

People say that there are freedom fighters who are like djinns, made of pure passion. In Islam, Allah creates the djinns before humans. Djinns are made of smokeless fire and are pure passion and no reason. Someone once said to me, 'When you are fighting an enemy as big as India for your freedom, you cannot do with humans. You need djinns.'

The metaphor seamlessly found its way into the story and, at the heart of it, the story became about the tussle between the djinn nature and the human nature of the people trapped in the conflict. I must admit that I am a huge fan of Tony Kushner's *Angels in America*, Shakespeare's *Macbeth*, Wole Soyinka's *Death and the King's Horseman* and Paula Vogel's *How I Learned to Drive*. I have always believed that ghosts hold the key to unlock our internal psyche in the most poetic way in a play. In a way, I wanted to add my own ghosts to the oeuvre of playwrights.

A metaphor can immensely animate a play. It can open up a plot and enable unity of action, time and space at a much deeper level that merely a unity of plot can.

An exercise in structure

Djinns of Eidgah went through several drafts, but the most radical changes were in its first four drafts when its structure was being shaped. The play from the beginning had four layers of narrative and two major timelines. These can be precisely articulated here as follows:

Layer 1: The story of siblings Ashrafi and Bilal. Ashrafi is a young girl and needs to come to terms with her trauma through the play as she keeps seeing and talking to a djinn. She does not know her objective, but I do. Bilal is her older brother. He wants to get through an important football trial and get out of Kashmir to play for a club in Brazil. He has to avoid getting sucked into the protests against the armed forces. He and I both know his objectives.

Layer 2: Dr Baig, Ashrafi's psychiatrist, is in his fifties and wants to heal Ashrafi. He also needs to read the *fateha* (the prayer for the dead) for his slain son Junaid, who had become a militant and given himself the name of Pareen. He and I both know his first objective, but he is in denial about his objective of reading the prayer at Junaid's grave because Baig has to accept Pareen in order to set Junaid free.

This gives me two options. Either he can accept his son at the end of some act and read the prayer later, after solving some other issue of the play, or he can accept his son and read the prayer at the same time. If the second thing happens, it has to be the last thing in the play. You cannot exorcise the djinn of *Djinns of Eidgah* and have more to say.

Layer 3: Junaid/Pareen needs to get his father to read the *fateha*. He does not know this, I know this.

He also wants Bilal to participate in the protests. Both of us know this.

He is also the djinn that Ashrafi talks to and no one else can see him. Ashrafi and I know this. This also makes Ashrafi, the patient, know more than Dr Baig, her doctor.

Layer 4: Two Indian soldiers, S1 and S2, who are trapped in their checkpost near the Eidgah. They cannot shoot at the stone-throwers for the fear of being lynched, but they have also been abandoned by their unit so they do end up shooting at the young boys. This will escalate tensions and derail the peace talks with the government.

S1 and S2 find out everything bit by bit. The audience finds out everything slightly ahead of them through other characters. The playwright has to know who in the play knows what and when very well. Otherwise, the release of information will be ad hoc and not in doses that help the dramatic build.

Timeline 1: Three days and two nights spanning Bilal's football trial, Eid, a boy's funeral and the peace talks. Thankfully, the Indian government in real life too has this tendency to pile up everything together to make most out of occasions for media coverage. It helps dramatic unity!

Timeline 2: Ashrafi and the djinn move back and forth in time in their surreal world. A boy who has been killed by the forces is about to join their world. This allows us to create backstories and scenes of suspension, and also reflect on the situation of the play outside the real timeline.

In the first draft, the narrators of the play were Hafiz and Rafis, two djinns. They took the play to the past, present and future. The play was filled with their presence as they brought these different strands together.

I was deeply attached to the two djinns. People who read the first draft loved its form. However, they were uncertain about the story. This is when Elyse asked me to do something that felt shocking: she asked me to write the second draft of *Djinns of Eidgah* without the djinns! She said that it would clarify the many strands of the story.

The second draft forced me to clarify the story. I was forced to confront the real arcs and plots of each character without the formal flourish.

It was after this, in the third draft, that I added the djinns back in and made the doctor's son Junaid the same djinn that Ashrafi keeps seeing.

The important thing to remember is that in Islam, people cannot die and become djinns. These are separate ideas. However, Rizwaan Khan, the caretaker of the martyr's graveyard in Srinagar, told me once sitting in the graveyard facing the Ali Masjid: 'The conflict has mashed up not only our lives but also our deaths. This is why the djinns of Ali Masjid keep calling the *ruh* (soul) of the martyrs.' I took a strand from this conversation to conflate the ideas. This line is said by Junaid to his father Dr Baig when he asks his son how could he become a djinn after dying.

This exercise of writing down separately the layers and timelines of the play has helped me often to construct multinarrative plays. I recommend this exercise before every draft for the writer to know exactly what are they about to try. The structure frees up the imagination. I find it very liberating.

Politics

It is extraordinarily important in any play to be able to articulate one's own politics around the theme. *Djinns of Eidgah* is based on three primary political ideas I developed while writing it.

The first is that the movement in Kashmir is a freedom struggle. Kashmir does not belong to India or Pakistan. Indians by and large believe that it is a Pakistan-based conspiracy. Pakistan has a role to play in supporting the insurgency undoubtedly, but the Kashmir issue is about right to self-determination. This is also why I have the chapters on Kashmir in the part 'Away' and not 'Home'.

The second is that Islam has really many different ideas. There are many differences in what Islam stands for within Kashmir. Understandably, as with every other religion, within a family there are differences about what it means and stands for. The fallout of 9/11 is that the world has learnt about Islam in a big way from George Bush, Osama bin Laden and Mohammad Atta. Atta held a master's degree in urban planning from the University of Hamburg. Osama was an MBA graduate and George Bush, I strongly believe, is uneducated (not illiterate, many illiterate people I know are immensely educated). None of them ever went to an Islamic school and yet Islam has been held responsible for terrorism. Madrasas and Islamic education have become a taboo. *Djinns of Eidgah* had to argue for the plurality in Islam and attempt to dispel some of the myths that have been paraded around it due to the world events of the last two decades.

Lastly, the movement in Kashmir is manifold. The students who throw stones are not from a militant group. Lashkar-e-Taiba, Hizbul Mujahideen, Al-Qaeda and others are all different groups with different agendas. Indian media has often clubbed all movements from Kashmir as terrorism. Several journalists, activists and children have been arrested and killed in the name of protecting the state from terrorists. I wanted the play to counter the myth of a homogenous hostile population.

Djinns of Eidgah has had several productions around the world. It has been taught and performed in many festivals, universities and venues in India, the United Kingdom, the United States and so on.

However, for me, two moments felt the most reassuring. The first was meeting Bhavani Basheer, the grand old man of Kashmiri theatre in Srinagar. Basheer Sahab had translated the play to Kashmiri and was about to stage it when the Covid-19 pandemic stopped all activity. Basheer Sahab's troupe making this play its own has meant a lot to me. I cannot wait to see it in Kashmiri.

The second moment was to meet Peter Brook in the audience in London. During the interval, Michael Billington and Peter Brook came to meet Richard Twynman, the director, and me in Elyse's office. I was so nervous I had two glasses of wine within those fifteen minutes. I have no idea what the second half of the play was like!

At the end of the play, he met us again and said, 'When the Greeks were making their tragedies, I believe something like what happened today in the theatre would have happened in their theatres.' I was flattered to say the least. I regret being so nervous that I never took his autograph or clicked a picture with him.

However, the next day, Peter and his wife, Natasha (a fabulous actress I worked with briefly in another residency), sent our team an email, which I will always cherish.

Never had I imagined, while loitering and reading in buses in Delhi during my college days, that one day this hunch in my head about Kashmir would take me to Bhavani Sahab and Peter Brook. I am indebted to the theatre for many such moments.

Djinns of Eidgah was shut down in India by the police in 2019 during a performance. Some right-wing goons had protested against it, and the play was stopped under a draconian theatre censorship law from Queen Victoria's time in 1876. There were threats against me and our company. The goons stormed into the theatre and blackmarked our names and our poster. Death threats were issued against me.

My wife and I did not send our daughter to school for a few days after the papers published that her father's play had been called seditious and anti-national.

In the following six months, theatre groups around the country performed it everywhere. In theatres, terraces, parks and drawing rooms. The staging of the play became a mini-revolt. This is the power of the theatre. The more one tries to stop it, the more it grows.

IV

Gasha

The Kashmir trilogy did not start out as being one. I never imagined while making *Rizwaan* that there would be other parts. However, after making *Rizwaan* and *Djinns of Eidgah* it was evident that one part was missing. The story of the Kashmiri Pandits who are upper-caste Hindus and who had to flee from the valley around 1989–91. As the first insurgency had picked up in Kashmir, death threats were issued against many Pandits. Many Pandits were prominent teachers and civil servants. Several of them had been killed by militants.

It led to a point where overnight people left their houses and escaped when they would suddenly come to know that a death threat had been issued against them.

In a spine-chilling incident, a man escaped from Srinagar with his wife and children overnight without telling his mother and older brother. He experienced such an atmosphere of distrust that he decided to not even tell his own family and trusted that the mother would be fine with the other brother's family. When he was in the car escaping with his family at night, he saw his other brother's family in a different vehicle. Both brothers had escaped with their families. The mother was left behind. The truth is that both brothers believed that the other would never leave Kashmir.

For several years, Kashmiri Pandits had lived in exile. Rebuilt their lives from scratch and always believed that in six to eight months they were going back home. These few months went on to become more than two decades. The Hindus had to escape. The army went in to Kashmir and the rest is the history of the conflict.

There is hardly any theatre that captures the trauma of this period. Since *Rizwaan* and *Djinns of Eidgah* were made, I thought here was an inevitable call for the play on the Pandits.

Adhir Bhat, who had acted in *Djinns of Eidgah* as a Kashmiri separatist, had once told me how strong and important he felt his role was. On the one hand, the character he was playing, Mushtaq, defended Kashmiri separatism. And on the other, Adhir himself had had to flee from Kashmir at the age of nine as a Hindu when his family was threatened by someone who had the same political opinions and demography as Mushtaq.

We spoke about developing a monologue with his family's story of exodus as an anchor for the play. In this he was to play himself and members of his family. He readily agreed and told me this would be challenging for him because he had lived the trauma of the exile. At one level he did not want to revisit it, and on the other, as a theatre actor, he knew it was also going to be his best chance to understand that trauma and share his story with the world.

Next on team was the brilliant writer and now my long-term collaborator Irawati Karnik. I had written and directed *Rizwaan*, written but not directed *Djinns of Eidgah* and here was an opportunity to direct in a devising process but not write the piece. I have always been excited about the possibility of doing different things in the theatre. It is one of my main draws to it. I find the strictness about writers not directing and vice versa in some theatre cultures unnecessarily restrictive. I think an artist only grows by being able to play the role they feel they want to in a project, as long as they are competent in it and their theatre culture allows this freedom.

As a first step, Ira and I conducted a workshop in Bangalore for ten days with Adhir. We were engaged in Adhir's story as an anchor and trying to create a structure around it. We mapped his journey from his childhood in Kashmir to having to leave overnight. We had small scenes from his school, home, life with friends and so on. We thought we had our structure and the play was going to be about how he left.

With ideas from this workshop, we met Anmol Vellani (director, philosopher, founder of the India Foundation for the Arts), who has been one of our chief mentors. After listening to the whole story patiently, he thought for some time and asked a simple question, 'So what?'

It was a blunt and brutal question to which we had no answer. Yes, we had an interesting narrative, but really – so what? We had a set of things to say but had no point of view.

What followed then on was a quest for a point of view. This quest is a vital ingredient in any work, especially documentary work. A theatre-maker can create a narrative, but the point of view informs every aspect of the production. One can argue that it is impossible to not have a point of view in any case, but it is possible for it to not be developed and therefore not translate to the production.

We went back to Kashmir. This time as a team compromising of Adhir, Ira, me and our dramaturg Subhasim Goswami, a sociologist. We went to Kheer Bhawani, which is the primary place of worship of the Pandits. Adhir's family organizes a large puja (a Hindu prayer ceremony) in the temple to which his entire extended family arrives from all over the world. All of them returning temporarily from their exile. The return has often been joyous and traumatic at the same time. We interviewed them extensively. It had been years since many of them had narrated the story of their exile. By now their memory was coloured by their personality and experience of life outside this traumatic experience.

After these interviews, we spoke to those Pandits who had stayed back in Kashmir and not left their houses. The Kashmiri Pandits by and large were extremely excited about us making a play on their experiences. They displayed an enormous amount of generosity and an urgency to be able to tell their story. A story they felt had gotten lost in the story of the larger Kashmir conflict. They took confidence in the fact that someone who had experienced the exile first-hand was going to act.

I have seen on many occasions communities owning plays even more if one of them is on stage. The trauma of one's trauma going unacknowledged in the world is so great that I believe it is extremely healing for a community to just see one of them in the powerful position of the storyteller. The history of civilization can be viewed as the history of people losing their right to be their own narrators. People trust the theatre because it can undo at least some wrongs in an immediate sense, by giving them an opportunity to tell their history through their narrator.

Next, we lived with a Muslim family in Srinagar and interviewed several other Muslim friends of mine whom I knew from previous trips. We also interviewed those Muslim families who had had Hindu neighbours.

There are distinctly two stories about the exile of the Pandits in Kashmir. The Hindus by and large believe that this was a betrayal by their Muslim neighbours. Many Muslims believe that it was a betrayal by the Hindus and that they were helped by the government to leave so that the army could come in and attack the Muslims. However, almost everyone irrespective of their religion believe that it was a dark time. And that Kashmir as a whole paid a huge price for that time.

By the time we left Kashmir, Adhir had seen many parts of Srinagar which he had not seen in twenty-five years. What was clear was that almost everything that we know about Hindus and Muslims in Kashmir was incomplete. It also became clear that one could not tell the story of the Hindus without including the position of their Muslim neighbour. That essentially it was a story of lost love and it had to have both.

As far-right groups on both sides continuously stoke fires of hatred, common people know that the moment the Pandits left was also the moment when Kashmir ceased to be a freedom movement and started to be portrayed as a religious fundamentalist issue.

The play took another year and multiple workshops to make. We worked with Ira's drafts over this time in both rehearsal and outside much in the same way that *Rizwaan* was worked upon. *Gasha* went on to perform for several years and received several awards including Best Script, Best Production and Best Ensemble (for its two actors, Adhir Bhat and Sandeep Shikhar) at the Mahindra Excellence in Theatre Awards in India. It initiated several conversations over these years and very often after the show we would meet Pandits and Muslims from Kashmir backstage. Some of them would hold Adhir and cry. Some would hold Sandeep and stand quietly. It was an experience that taught me a lot about how long should a company stay in the theatre before leaving for the night when they are performing a play that means so much to a community. Sometimes we had to go to people's houses to eat because they had more to tell us about the trauma. It changed our lives in many ways.

Rizwaan, *Djinns of Eidgah* and *Gasha* together played for a decade in India and had multiple shows in other countries by different groups. All of them chronicled Kashmir through the eyes of children. These plays also were the first in which I had to leave home and make something elsewhere with stories of people who had other lives and other contexts. Stories in which our collaboration as a community and a theatre-maker became crucial.

This became in some sense the foundation of my theatre-making in the world thereon, apart from all the theatre I make in Indian languages in India. I had come to the theatre to find a way of understanding the world. The trilogy gave me the people, friends, collaborators, resilience, joy and learnings to start to move out of my comfort zone and try to understand the world through the theatre.

V

Postscript

I was sitting with Irfan Hasan in a coffee shop in Srinagar. December 2010. Irfan Hasan was a close friend of Agha Shahid's. He was in the police several years ago and had resigned from it after an unfair crackdown on Kashmiris by the police. I was telling him about the letter in *Rizwaan* that was at the centre of the book and had formed the heart of the play.

He went quiet and asked me if I could come the next day. I told him of course I could come. I had come to interview him. I could meet him every day if he wanted to.

The next day, he met me at the same coffee shop with an old fax in his hand. It was the same letter with a few different words. It was Irfan's. Irfan had informed Agha Shahid about Rizwaan's death through that letter. Rizwaan was their common friend's younger brother and quite close to Agha Shahid.

Agha Shahid had changed some of the words to include the letter in the book. I could not believe I had accidentally met the man who started this entire journey for me.

Rizwaan had crossed the border. He was in a camp to train to fight the Indian armed forces. On the way back, he was shot dead and he did indeed die bleeding on the snow. Irfan Hasan and I remain friends till today. We still meet up in Kashmir. Drink coffee. Walk. And discuss poetry. I still cannot believe I am walking with the man who wrote that letter to Shahid.

Adhir, Ira and I met my friend Showkat Motta in Srinagar. Showkat is a very well-known editor in Kashmir who is known to be non-compromising. Initially, the conversation was general and cautious. Both Adhir and Showkat were discussing the exile of Pandits carefully. Showkat is a Kashmiri Muslim and very few people have chronicled Kashmir better than he has.

As the conversation developed, they realized that as children they used to go to the same paediatrician. They remembered the doctor, the house and the plants outside. They embraced and held the embrace. In the room there was a strange sense of completion. Of having met a brother after twenty-five years. That something vital had been lost in these years. That this meeting too could last only this long.

For me, *Gasha* was all about that embrace. It's difficulties and its desire.

Sometimes an entire play can be about one gesture between two people that has been denied through history outside the theatre.

These are the gestures for which I believe people trust the theatre.

These are the moments in which the inner life of people exists on stage while their fiction is out there, in the so-called 'real' world.

6

The writing of *Pah-la*

A theatre journey across the roof of the world

I

India and early research

There are very few experiences for me that will ever match again the experience of writing *Pah-la*. This play has been one of the most demanding things I have ever done in my life. I knew that it was going to be an unusual play to write, but I do not think that even in its first two years I had any idea of what was going to come.

Pah-la, which means father in Tibetan, is a play, which started with the question 'What is the future of non-violence?'

I started thinking about this question after my Kashmir plays and also after a play called *Afterlife of Birds* for which I had interviewed ex-members of the Sri Lankan Liberation Tigers of Tamil Eelam (LTTE) in Europe. Years of spending time around people who were involved in these revolutions made me aware to a large extent about the nuances and multiple positions that people occupy in these movements. It also increasingly seemed to me that the world had accepted armed revolutions as the only form of legitimate large-scale protest.

In early twentieth century, there had been a historical moment in which there were several burgeoning non-violent moments. Gandhi in South Africa and India had gone on to inspire Martin Luther King and Mandela. By and large, the decolonization of the African continent post-1950s had been non-violent. In India, the mighty British Empire had been made to see the power of a people's movement by people who had no other ammunition than a moral premise. Sceptics have said that it was not the non-violent movement per se that led to the decolonization by the British but the economic distress of the Second World War, and while this is partly true and an attractive radical view, I am not in agreement with it. There are several documents from the British parliament from the pre–Second World War period that reveal that the push for independence of India had started earlier than the war.

At the same time, there were several people in the British administration who were extremely uncomfortable with the idea of decolonizing in the first place. We have to take into account the fact that the British ruled India for nearly two hundred years. This means that several generations of British citizens had been born into the false premise of colonial supremacy and, worse still, colonial benevolence.

Since the mid-1940s, I do not think we have seen another fundamental change of that scale in the world. Eradication of poverty, universal health care, access to justice or education has not achieved the degree of change that decolonization as a phenomenon achieved in the mid-twentieth century. Pankaj Mishra in his book *From the Ruins of Empire: The Intellectuals Who Remade Asia* argues rightly that while the West believes the central event of the world in the last century to be the two world wars, it was in fact decolonization that deserves to rightly take that mantle because it impacted a much larger population than the wars. In fact, much of these two wars were also fought by the colonized people on behalf of their colonial masters. This large-scale decolonization movement had in its ranks several major non-violent leaders and populations, who when faced with guns and batons did not give up on the moral premise of their belief. However, by the time we get to the end of the twentieth century, this reality is lost to the world.

There is almost no major large-scale freedom movement that can claim the position of non-violence. This seems completely counter-intuitive if one compares the success of the mid-twentieth-century movements to the ones later. At the same time, it also points to the reality that the colonizers of the neocolonial world, often the colonized in the last centuries, have left no room for non-violent struggle against them even though they might have achieved their freedom through the same means.

The exception to this is the Tibetan struggle.

Since the 1950s, the Tibetan struggle is known to have been by and large non-violent. His Holiness the Dalai Lama was in fact inspired by Gandhi himself to give up the means of the Chushi Gangdruk, a guerrilla force that fought the PLA in the mid-1900s. They were trained by the CIA and were extremely tough Tibetan warriors who made the occupation of Tibet by Chinese forces quite difficult despite large disparity in the size and resources between these two armies.

Once His Holiness called the movement off, it turned completely non-violent. Tibetans worldwide, for half a century, have been the most vocal proponents of non-violence. At the same time, they have obviously also held on steadfastly to the belief that the might of the Chinese state will eventually crumble and they will have freedom.

This last great bastion of non-violence is what drew me to it. I was curious about my central question and thought that this would be the right place to examine it.

I had also had several Tibetan friends while I was studying in Delhi University. In fact, very close to Delhi University is a locality which is primarily a Tibetan area, and Delhi University students have been regulars in the little cafes and restaurants there for years.

I decided to begin by developing a process that involved interviewing Tibetans-in-exile living in India and by reading across three broad subjects.

First, my reading was around the story of Tibet before the formation of the People's Republic of China. Second, the story after. And third, about Mahayana Buddhism in general and within that Tibetan Buddhism specifically. I spent two years reading through a wide syllabus on these subjects. In parallel, I was interviewing Tibetans-in-exile. In McLeod Ganj and Dharamshala in Himachal Pradesh, a mountain state in India, where the Tibetan government in exile is located and where His Holiness the Dalai Lama lives. And also, in Bangalore and Bylakuppe, in the southern state of Karnataka, where a large number of Tibetans live.

My philosophy when it comes to interviewing people for plays comprises three simple principles. First, that they should know what they are being interviewed for. Second, I should not write or record anything as they are speaking. Third, that our real interview will begin when we meet the third or fourth time or when we share a meal or drink tea at someone's house. Before that happens in my view nothing worth having in a play is found. There are many people in a person. What I am looking for is not information, I am looking for *shared presence*. I also do not interview before reading extensively. The background is my responsibility. The person being interviewed should feel that they can tell me what they feel or free-associate, rather than have to recreate facts in a linear manner. That kind of interview for the purpose of my plays is quite useless in my view.

The theatre is not the best place to dramatize events. It is the best place to manifest one's deeper psychology and feelings. The events are only the excuse on which the feelings will sit in a play. The reportage on them is available quite extensively on other media that deal exclusively with reporting matters.

As I interviewed for a long time, I could sense that there is a deep story that I am not getting much access to. That somehow there was a roadblock which seemed to not be able to take us to that realm of the deeper answers and questions. Partly, I think it was because of language. Most people I was speaking to were primarily speakers of Tibetan language. And memory stores different kinds of thoughts in different languages. English or Hindi might not have been for them the language to unpack their personal stories and images.

This changed in the second summer in McLeod Ganj in Himachal Pradesh in India. McLeod Ganj is a beautiful Himalayan town in India, full of Tibetan families and also the main temple and residence of HH the Dalai Lama.

I was here with Priyanka Krishna, who was assisting me in research. She was by and large interviewing the nuns and I was working on interviewing monks and others of non-monastic orders.

In the summer, several Buddhists from around the world come to McLeod Ganj for additional classes in Buddhism. Monks from Thailand, Sri Lanka, Burma and Vietnam are also seen often, although they might be from completely different orders. There are also Tibetan Buddhist monks who visit for advanced classes. During these times, there are some institutes that look for English speakers to volunteer to teach English classes. I had signed up for some of these.

One of the methods of teaching, we were told, was to ask the person attending the class to pick up a slip from a bowl that had four or five words. Then the student would try to form sentences with these words and the job of the teacher would be to aid that conversation.

It was here that the process really opened up. Several Tibetans who had walked across the Himalayas to escape the Chinese government were coming to class every day. The associative words were leading them to talk about several deeply insightful details of their lives and their journeys. It is here that I met the people who would go on to frame a lot of the subsequent research. The first of them was a young monk called Dawa, who had grown up in exile in India and had gone through a non-monastic regular school and had graduated from a college in North India before going to monastic college.

Dawa and I sat every evening with tea in a terrace restaurant surrounded by mountains. Here we would discuss several aspects of Tibetan Buddhist philosophy, and we would engage in a series of discussion and debates around its principles. It is through these conversations that Dawa started to tell me about the various stories and reports he knew from inside Tibet. As we spoke evening after evening, the place of Buddhist philosophy in Tibetan life was becoming clearer to me. This is one of the most important things to understand about the Tibetan struggle. That at its heart is Buddhist belief. The question I had about the future of non-violence became inextricably linked with the future of Tibetan Buddhism. It was becoming very clear why the Dalai Lama had insisted on retaining educational, cultural and spiritual institutions in a struggle that otherwise seemed like it was for very physical and concrete things like land-rights and housing.

The second person who became very important for this research was Adam, which is not his real name.

Adam had escaped from Tibet to India in a third attempt. Twice he had been arrested very close to the border by the Chinese army and sent to jail.

He had an extraordinary story about how his grandfather wanted him to reach India in order to receive an education outside of the Chinese system. This theme eventually became a major part of the play. The imposition of Chinese education in Tibet is a major reason for people to escape from Tibet. In the early years of Chinese occupation, Mandarin was introduced in Tibetan schools as a language but all other subjects were taught in Tibetan. Now only Tibetan language classes are in Tibetan and everything else is taught in Mandarin in most places.

Some of the world's most treasured Buddhist scriptures exist only in Tibetan. To lose this language is to lose some of the greatest advancements in human history. Adam became my primary source to learn about the route from Shigatse that most people who escaped took. The entire network of guides there, who have enabled many of these escapes in groups, is a play unto itself. Adam became my entry point into that network. This walk across the Himalayas has been well documented in several films and books. It is unreal that in the twenty-first century, there have been thousands of people who have had to walk across the mighty Himalayas, at heights which the greatest climbers would find unnerving, with old people and children in order to escape the Chinese regime. I have not known of a single group in which everyone has ever reached the other side. Adam attempted this life-threatening walk not once, not twice but thrice. That is how desperate his grandfather – a teacher and an ex-soldier in the Tibetan struggle – was to get him out of Tibet and send him to India where he could learn in Tibetan in Tibetan schools.

The third very important person was and continues to be is Lhakpa Tsering. Lhakpa is the director of a theatre group called Tibet Theatre based out of Dharamshala. Lhakpa had escaped from Tibet as a child and reached India's easternmost borders. He was raised in exile in India at the Tibetan Children's Village (TCV, another brainchild of His Holiness). In 2006, Lhakpa had set himself on fire in front of the Taj Hotel in Mumbai in protest against the Chinese president Hu Jintao, who was at that time visiting India and staying in the hotel.

Lhakpa is both a revolutionary and a theatre director. He is now also the translator of *Pah-la* in Tibetan and will be directing it in 2022 as part of an Indian-Tibetan-German collaboration. This Tibetan production with Tibetan actors will be touring several countries starting 2022.

Priyanka meanwhile had found some invaluable information from the interviews she was conducting with the nuns. There were some questions already coming up during our research. We must have interviewed about fifty people in and around McLeod Ganj and overall more than two hundred Tibetans of different age groups and ethnic groups in these two years. Although many of them had come from Tibet at some point of time or the other, it was becoming clear that since 2008 this traffic had significantly reduced. It had become almost impossible to escape from Tibet post-2008.

I had also started to get into chat sites which had both Tibetan and Chinese participants. Earlier I tried to access some of those in Chinese language and translate it online, but eventually I had to rely more on the ones which were active internationally and in which at least one of the primary languages of communication was English.

During this online research, it was also becoming clear that something had happened post-2008 to the security systems so that escape had now become impossible. The Tibetan border with India and Nepal is a long one. It is also hard terrain and it's impossible to man every inch of it. Yet the level of security had gone up considerably. In 2008, there was a large-scale protest in Lhasa. This had led to a massive crackdown on Tibetans by the Chinese authorities. This protest of 2008 also was unlike anything in recent history. It was large scale and varied. It was also spontaneous. There were large sections of non-violent protests. There were also some pockets of violence.

Most importantly, the protests were extremely successful in putting immense pressure on the Chinese authorities.

In about forty years, the Chinese authorities had not had to ask for additional companies of soldiers to come in to Lhasa. The Han population in Lhasa has in any case grown ever since the Beijing to Lhasa train has come into the picture and also the government has given huge incentives for people from Mainland China to come and settle in Tibet. However, I found out later that there were additional soldiers needed this time.

It had also been a potent opportunity by the Chinese authorities to discredit the narrative around the non-violent nature of the Tibetan movement.

As I followed the internet trail, more information started to come out, and it became obvious that any serious leads about the Chinese response to 2008 would not be available in the public domain. I would need to connect to some serious hackers to get through some Chinese websites, systems and firewall in order to get concrete information.

Thankfully, Bangalore is hacker heaven. It is one of the world's largest IT hub, and there are several hacker clubs in Bangalore who hack as a serious hobby. I went to a university in South India which had some brilliant hacking minds even while I was there. I am not a computer-science person, but in the past, I had helped some of my friends with some mathematical solutions for algorithms they needed to test. I got in touch with some of those friends and we started getting into databases and servers.

Two very important discoveries were made during this research. One was that Hong Kong Police had sold polygraph machines to police in Tibet post-2008. In large numbers. In general, the prison equipment in Tibet had gone up considerably. Tibet has some of the world's most notorious prisons. Particularly Chushur and Drapchi close to Lhasa. They are mega-facilities and particularly Chushur has grown manifold post-2008.

A large amount of the equipment had gone to these two prisons.

The second discovery was that there is an online system of passing codes in the Tibetan struggle from within Mainland China that uses the internet very effectively. I will refrain from placing the method in public domain here. However, it became clear that the picture that we had of Tibet from outside was grossly incomplete and based on terribly old models of seeking information.

In any modern state, people are aware of a small pie of the workings of the state. Human testimonial is paramount to finding out what people feel and experience. However, the trail of hard information is online. If we are to look for people, we have to look for satellite data. And if we have to look for what people are doing, we have to look carefully at what are they doing on the internet. What are they buying or selling, what are the adverts, which trades are occurring frequently in both the business-to-consumer and the business-to-business sectors.

The writing of *Pah-la* revealed to me that the Chinese state is not opaque but translucent.

What also became clear is that this play could not be written by interviewing Tibetans-in-exile alone. To answer the question of 'What is the future of non-violence?' one obviously had to look inside Tibet. That is where it is hardest to remain non-violent. That is where something major had happened. That is where Chinese prison guards had left service after 2008 and gone back to their homeland. That is where there were reports of a satellite firewall being built as early as 2010 that could monitor the mountain range so that any movement could be traced right away. This is now in place in 2021.

I started speaking online to two groups of people now. The first were the contacts of Tibetans-in-exile who were still in Tibet and had been there in 2008. Second were the leads I had in Beijing of ex-police workers in Lhasa. All of them had resigned. Even if I would be able to meet one of them, I could potentially have more leads to follow up in Lhasa.

It also became clear that I would have to take the Beijing-Lhasa express in order to get a sense of this enormous contributor to the change in Tibet. Hence what would need to be done was to get to Beijing and from there to Lhasa in order to do some of these interviews. And these would need to be done with no trail. No paper, nothing recorded or typed inside China.

At the same time, the meetings would be too precious to be not made a note of as they were happening. So, I had to devise two systems. The first would be a system of writing that would give me the information in a way that I could decipher it or remember it once back in India, and the second would be a way of creating a map of Lhasa on which I could map out which localities had been affected in what way in 2008.

This is vital to understanding 2008. It is true that it was a serious large-scale protest. It is also true that it was a riot. It depends on which part of the city one was looking at. Like most cities in the world, Lhasa has also got ghettoized over the years. There are sections of the city where the ordinary people stay, and there are places where bureaucrats and people of power and wealth stay. The extent of police aggression and the degree of retaliation were relatively very different in these areas for reasons of density and overall sense of social injustice in my view. When I interviewed people in these different areas, it was very clear that Lhasa is not unlike most capitals. Its urbanization has been more rapid than that of most megapolises of the world. The influx of a large number of Han people into Lhasa is well known specially after the train.

I devised a way of making the map by drawing the map of Lhasa rotated by 55 degrees and superimposing a map of Delhi on top in my notebook. As I marked the map no one would know what city was being marked and at the same time I would be able to see what kind of patterns emerge across the city. I learnt this technique too from the theatre. Several years ago, I had attended a theatre workshop at the Puppet Theatre Barge in London. There we had learnt how to make the night sky for a puppet show. That it had to be based on the real picture of the night sky and also at the same time it would need to suit our needs. Hence, we had superimposed one image on another. I used the same method in my map of Lhasa.

Pallavi, my wife, and I decided to go together. I was going in to interview people who were consensual interviewees, and I knew that there was nothing illegal about it. Thankfully, at that time, we did not have each other's names on our passports. Hence, this was useful to the extent that it would ensure that if I was caught at any point of time, there would essentially be no trace to hold her back. She could just come back from there and do what was needed from India. But to be honest, we did not think it was going to be all that dangerous. After all, I was to meet some people in their houses and talk. People who had all been verified twice over. Also, people who were all referred by others, who I knew quite well by now and who had some connection to an actual person in India.

It took two and half years to prepare for this trip to Lhasa.

By now His Holiness the Dalai Lama's the Foundation for Universal Responsibility was on board. They supported the research without any caveats. I was open to write anything I wanted. I was to find out for myself what was true or not about Tibet and write the play. No questions asked.

Thanks to them and Elyse Dodgson at the Royal Court Theatre, this trip could happen. Elyse was the champion of new writing in the world. She stood by this play and several other plays which would have never seen the light of day in the world if not for her. She also stood by them knowing that they might never work out. They might not turn out to be as good as their proposals, or even if they did, they might turn out to be unstageable within the restrictions of the Royal Court Theatre in terms of form and programming capacity. Yet she stood by them like a rock. When I told her that I was going in to Tibet to research, she asked me if I was sure. I said that I was and she just told me to be careful.

Pallavi and I left for Beijing via Hong Kong. I think it was a very late-night flight. We were asleep. My diary was in the bag. Which no one else in the world could read except me. And yet it did not look like code. It just looked like another language and another city's map.

The theatre had taught me this. To be able to transpose reality. To be able to travel. To get lost in a crowd and most importantly to do what is needed to tell a story that needs to be told.

II

Beijing

To get a visa to Beijing, we had to submit an itinerary. An itinerary which detailed what we were planning to do every single day of the stay. Not just every day but each half of the day.

We had to mention which places we were planning to visit. Which museums, monuments, parks and historical sites would be on our list and when exactly. On arriving, we were to be met with a guide at the airport. She was responsible to take us to all these places. She was also responsible for ensuring that we actually did what we had put down in the itinerary. At the end of the week in Beijing, we would catch the Beijing-Lhasa express to Lhasa.

Never before had I been to a place where it is obligatory to be where I had promised. If we said that at 4.00 pm on Tuesday we were going to go to the Forbidden City, we had to. One could not fall ill, lose interest or change plan. The guide was as much a tourist-advisor as someone with duties to ensure complete surveillance.

(From here on in this chapter, I will change names. This is mainly because this information can be very damaging for some of the people. The ones I have consent from will be written about in totality.)

Our guide took us to our hotel. It was a comfortable old hotel, which at one point of time had been home to aristocrats. Although it had the wear and tear of time, it was still beautiful.

We checked in. Rested for some time and I left in the evening for my first interview. This had been coordinated from Bangalore. The person knew which hotel I was going to be in and had come to meet me. We sat in a small tea shop close by, which was more like the back of a house than a proper shop. His name was Han and was a friend of someone I had known from Dharamshala. He had spent some years working in the police force in Lhasa. In 2009, he had quit the service. He had first gone to his hometown and then he had come over to

Beijing to make a living. He had served in Tibet for four years. It was hard for him to adjust but the perks of serving in Tibet were greater.

However, by the end of his term he had a superior who was 'inhuman'. His word. Someone who would be completely unpredictable in a stressful situation. It sometimes appeared, he told me, that this superior used to get a high from the violence. He spoke to me about 2008. About the chaos in Lhasa at that time. No one even clearly knew what started it. Some said it was connected to protests timed around the Beijing Olympics and to create a major humanitarian crisis when the world was looking at China. We spoke till late evening and in this time, he said several contradictory things about Tibetans. This was quite understandable since he had actually served in Tibet. He had seen criminals who were Tibetan and had also served alongside Tibetans. Like a soldier from any occupying force, he had his dilemmas about the execution of the programme but very little doubt about the importance of it. He had no doubt that Tibet had become a better place because of the presence of the Chinese government. The material development was unprecedented, but he said that as time was going by, many people in the forces were forgetting what the original intent was and were misusing power. He had many Tibetan friends, and he was surprised that several Tibetans continued to serve under that inhuman superior while he had quit despite being a Han.

He had also set up two more meetings for me in the days to come. One of them was with another Han and the other with a Tibetan. He asked me a lot of questions about the Hindi-film industry and I answered to the best of my ability. The Hindi-film industry has led me to interviews outside India more than once. Many people think that if a person who writes plays comes from India, he must ultimately be connected to Hindi films that several people love.

I had to disappoint him on that front, but I thought it was a good start.

The next day onwards, mornings and evenings were completely different. In the morning, we would step out for sightseeing and our guide would take us around, following the itinerary like a promise. Our tickets to Lhasa were still not confirmed, and I had called my agent in India. He could not explain himself why it was so.

There are two kinds of seats in the train. Hard seat and soft seat. He told me that for some reason we were booked in one hard and one soft seat in two different compartments. I had no idea why this was the case and who had done the booking in Beijing.

On the third evening, I felt one of my meetings go wrong. The lady I was interviewing had left Tibet to come back to Beijing but I think somewhere in the interview she started to think that I was going to be writing against the Chinese police officers. I realized it and tried to explain to her that I had no predetermined loyalty, but she seemed to turn hostile.

Next morning, our guide told us that our tickets to Lhasa were cancelled. That we could no longer take the train, and there was nothing that could be done about it.

I called our agent in India, and he was completely shocked by this development.

The only thing to be done, he said, was to catch the flight to Xining and pay a bribe there to get on to the train. The train that we were to take was going to reach Xining a day later. The other option was to stay on in Beijing for some more days and then go to some other part of China for a holiday at the same price. To drop Tibet from the itinerary.

We wrapped up Beijing and its interviews sooner than planned. We had to make sure that we would be able to get the train. In fact, we timed ourselves in such a way that we would reach Xining a day before our earlier arrival date there. That way we would have a chance to catch at least one of the trains if our bribing failed the first time. I managed to set this up with our agent.

A week after our arrival in Beijing, we left for Xining by a morning flight. A few hours later, we were in mountainous terrain. We had landed in Xining and a middle-aged Uighur man was our person there. He greeted us and we waited for hours for the Beijing-Lhasa express to arrive.

He said he would try the bribe once it was close to time, and they had a sense of how many seats are vacant. The bribe to the train supervisor gets fixed based on that.

III

Beijing-Lhasa express

Boarding the Beijing-Lhasa express was a dream come true. I had read so much about this, and it was such a site of contest in the history of Tibet that it was surreal to actually be on it. Pallavi too was extremely excited about making this journey. It is easily one of the most scenic train rides anywhere. The train goes up to heights from where the Everest can be seen and from there comes down to arrive at Lhasa city. At night, attendants come in and switch on additional oxygen supply in the compartments because of the dip in oxygen levels during the climb.

The train passes through the roof of the world. The Himalayas.

I have been in many train rides and car rides in the Himalayas in India but had experienced nothing like this. The size of the mountains and the vast expanse of sparsely populated places seem like one is floating on top of the clouds with hills protruding from below.

Passing through Tibet, I found my sense of scale and height changing. One feels so small. So insignificant in the scheme of things.

The sense of colour changes as well. In Tibet, the white of the sky is whiter than any conception I had ever had of that colour. It meets giant mountains which have snow of a completely different white. The clouds and snow roll down to meet blue lakes that can shatter glass with the reflection of light on them.

It is in the midst of these large sparse lands one can see in the middle of nowhere sometimes a Chinese soldier standing and saluting the train.

The image of these young men was one of the strongest introductions that I had to Tibet. A man alone in a uniform, guarding nothing but just symbolically standing up and saluting the train as if it were a person. Surrounded by miles and miles of mountains and nothingness, these people begin the symbolism of China in Tibet.

Then as we move closer to hamlets and villages, once in a while, there appear houses. Large houses that look all the same. Made of red bricks and with a Chinese flag on top.

The easiest way of identifying which is a government house in Tibet is this. The red flag. These houses are given on long-term loans. The government gives majority of the money and helps to construct them. The people who take these houses have to work and stay there for fifteen to twenty years. It is not the train alone but a series of such schemes that brought Han people in large numbers to Tibet. These reasons are wide and varied.

The train has a dining car and every compartment also has a hot-water tap for people to add hot water to their instant ramen. This is staple food on this train most of the times.

People from all walks of life were in our compartment. I spoke to some of the people in this train. They were workers, builders, teachers who were travelling in the cheaper compartment. The other compartment had relatively wealthy people. They had more privacy, their bathrooms were cleaner and they had a visibly different sense of space on the train. In the poorer compartment, no such thing as space was paid any attention to. Much like trains in India, we were at home with this arrangement.

It was wonderful to be amid all these people who were effortlessly mixing together. Han and Tibetans. This was their reality.

While interviewing people in exile, I could sense a deep pain at having to leave their home. Without anything most of the time.

Here, however, people were talking to each other and laughing.

This dichotomy is the nature of conflict in the world. No one person can stand for the conflict completely, and at the same time, it is not a story of two sides. It is a story of multiple sides and, most importantly, of common human condition. That most of the times we as ordinary people are no longer aware of the silent and strong oppression that we are under. Oppression in the modern age has the potential to make us like it. In earlier times, even indentured labour, while travelling to distant plantations to be sold by weight, were at least aware of the oppression they were escaping from and the one they were sailing into in slave ships. In modern times, the oppressed is made unaware of it. The oppressed celebrates personal material micro-successes as markers of culture while the culture at large comfortably exploits them in the name of personal agency and the bogey of merit. The oppressor introduces rituals and social pride while in parallel replacing dignity and personal sense of worth with large scale and multi-pronged propaganda.

This bombardment of propaganda is not a communist specialty as the West would have us believe. We have seen in recent times how false news and propaganda have led to the raiding of the so-called Mecca of liberty, the Capitol in Washington DC.

Modern life world over suffers from the incomprehension of what philosopher Timothy Morton calls 'hyperobjects' in his book *Hyperobjects: Philosophy and Ecology After the End of the World*. Hyperobjects are 'entities of such vast temporal and spatial dimensions that they defeat traditional ideas about what a thing is in the first place'. Writing in the context of ecology, Morton points to the modern phenomenon that has given rise to such large objects of connected entities that the common person can no longer see their shapes and sizes.

Modern oppression is one such hyperobject because it is inexhaustibly linked to nationalism, capitalism and fictional history. Unlike the colonizers of the sixteenth to early twentieth centuries, we are in a situation where the enemy or the oppressor is clouded in the propaganda of goodness that early colonizers were nascently developing. The lie of serving others by paternal governmental diktats is now a hyperobject in both the capitalist world and communist China.

The ride in that train, with two and half years of preparation behind it, made one thing very clear to me. That the Western media by and large was wrong about China. Just like multiple newspapers in Western democracies have opinion-pieces every weekend on how China is about to collapse, the same happens in China. Ten days in China is enough to make one feel that America is on the brink of collapsing completely. The reason Western cinema particularly infantilizes China is because it is unable to comprehend the hyperobject.

It is a communist state with the highest capital growth in the world.

It is a people's republic with no representation of people in large spheres of life. It is a country where people gather in parking lots in Beijing with coordination that one can only dream of elsewhere, to exercise in unison in the evenings when the government announces a 'fitness revolution'.

It has soldiers who do not shoot. Do not guard. Do not defend. They stand in the middle of nowhere to salute a train. The West infantilizes or exoticizes China in popular fiction because sitting in America, there is no comprehension of the other big nation that is challenging it with pretty much the opposite discourse.

What we do not understand, we worship or make fun of. It is a way to avoid reality.

My introduction to Tibet in real terms had started. It was not going to be simple. It was not going to be all of any one idea.

It was modern, intellectual, materialist and at the same time, traditional, superstitious and deeply philosophical. Just the kind of contradiction that reveals the human condition at its core. Pure theatre in action.

IV

Lhasa

The next afternoon, twenty-four hours after boarding the train in Xining, we reached Lhasa.

Writing about Lhasa is complicated. Largely for reasons of security. There are several people in Lhasa who contributed immensely to what unfolded thereon. However, Tibet is an extreme case of surveillance. The punishment for saying or doing anything that the Chinese government believes to be anti-national is severe.

Let me begin this section in memory of Rinzin, who was eight when I met him last. Three years later, he was starved to death in a Chinese prison. His fault was that his father had been arrested and was supposedly not revealing what he was being asked in the interrogation. No one knows what his father was actually arrested for. But he was part of a proto-revolutionary group, and my sense is that it could be something related to a burgeoning movement inside Tibet that we will see erupt within our lifetime in a big way.

I remember Rinzin vividly. I remember him for his gorgeous laughter. For his broken English and his beautiful Tibetan. We had to speak to each other through his uncle. I also remember Rinzin for his wisdom.

I pause here in his memory.

We got down at Lhasa station by late afternoon. At the station, all tourists were handed two pamphlets. Both were for musicals, one called *The Mighty Himalayas* and the second, *The Ballad of Princess Wencheng*. I was surprised, to say the least, to receive pamphlets of two musicals as the first markers of welcome in a city as rich with its own history of performative traditions as Lhasa.

However, very soon, I realized the importance of the pattern of symbols that had begun to appear from the moment of encountering the saluting guards on the mountain.

China is a large communist country. It takes pride in its advancements. In its material, technological and modern cultural feats. Its promise to Tibet is that of material advancement and all the symbolism is about this very promise.

It appeared extremely surprising to me that in the land of the Potala Palace, Jokhang Temple and Barkhor Square, two Chinese musicals should be foregrounded. In Kashmir, India still foregrounds the Mughal gardens and the Dal Lake. However, India occupies by assimilation and China by radical industrialization. Both are different skills. Both are completely different models derived to suit the identity of the occupier.

What is extremely important is to understand the symbolism of the story of Princess Wencheng. It is the story of a princess who married the Tibetan king Songsten Gampo. The Tibetans claim that King Gampo was Buddhist and Princess Wencheng brought a statue of Buddha as dowry. But the Chinese claim that it was Princess Wencheng who introduced Buddhism to Tibet.

This is a massive attempt to culturally claim that Tibet was always part of Mainland China, the stand which Tibetans will fight against till their last breath. Here is an example of the power of performance. The Chinese state's first propaganda in Lhasa is a Western-style musical. Tibet has a performance tradition that includes ballads and operas dating back to thousands of years. However, within any brochure, any printed matter or television advert for Tibet, the Chinese state shows no such performance. The singular pictures are of such Broadway-style musicals.

The Chinese state knows the power of performance. I should have realized this right there but it took me longer, and I learnt the hard way later as multiple attempts were being made to stop the staging of *Pah-la*.

One of the first things I learnt in Tibet is that it is forbidden to take the name of His Holiness the Dalai Lama. Yes. It is forbidden to say it.

The people are so aware of surveillance that he is referred to as 'HH'.

Conversation between Indians and Tibetans invariably goes in that direction. Tibet is also the only place I have been to in the world where Indians are silently welcomed as if one was going to someone's house. Tibetans are deeply aware of the fact that their god lives in our country. That our country takes enormous pride in him and loves him enormously.

To understand what the Dalai Lama has achieved, one has to only ask a simple question. Is there another man from any religion in the entire world who has had his popularity over so many years and yet has not a single controversy to his name?

There is no person of any other religion who holds anything against His Holiness. Him. That god is in our country.

Tibetans fold hands in street corners, in markets and from their houses to welcome Indians. I have never been this moved by a gesture of hospitality in any other place in the world.

I had my map, my meetings set up and an itinerary that we were obliged to follow. The same cycle started. Days of itinerary and late evenings of meetings and interviews.

Lhasa offers an enormous lot to a writer. Imagine a place where tourists are not allowed to meet locals for all practical purposes. All tourists had to travel in buses and cars with the letter 'L' on their number plates. One could not be seen in anything else.

I knew this before arriving there, and hence, all my meetings were arranged in specific areas where I could walk with the person who helped me take my interviews.

One night, I had two meetings within an hour in a modern bar. This bar was full of young people.

I met here an ex-monk who had been removed from his monastery by the Chinese government. The Chinese government had begun issuing licences to be monks. He was now without a licence. A licence to renounce surely sounded counter-intuitive. He spoke about 2008 and what happened when the protests started. It was also him who connected me to another man who arranged for a larger gathering the following evening in a tea room in someone's house.

This was not safe to start with. A place like Lhasa is teeming with Chinese agents. Like in Kashmir. There are people who cross lines not once but twice sometimes in order to report and counter-report others.

But something about our conversation in the bar made me think that he was telling the truth, and he was not an agent. I knew his brother in India but that was not the security. The security was that apart from mentioning the Chinese atrocities in 2008, he mentioned the shock at the incidents of Tibetan violence. He said to me, 'At one point of time, I thought I would kill someone. And why wouldn't I? I was not a monk anymore!'

He had not killed anyone. He was referring to the fact that the Chinese authorities had also used a lot of Tibetans to fight Tibetans. Heads of police who were Tibetans had been given the dirtiest of jobs. The most violent crackdowns on the protest were to be conducted by Tibetan officers and the scale was unthinkable. Especially till reinforcements arrived from elsewhere.

This use of Tibetans to attack Tibetans was unprecedented, and what was also unprecedented in some cases were the attacks on Chinese properties by Tibetans. In one case, on a primary school. 'Why would anyone attack a primary school?' he asked.

He said to me, 'I fear this violence the most. If we turn violent, the revolution is all over. If we are violent, there is no meaning in freedom.'

This sentence of his became the spine of the play.

World over, there is violence and civil unrest. Some elements from the weakest sections of societies engage in acts of violence, only to protect themselves.

However, in Tibet, this was unthinkable. Tibetans have vowed under His Holiness the Dalai Lama to not get violent. They are religious people. Religion is at the heart of the struggle. How could they turn violent even in an off-incident – this was his question.

The next day, I went into the tea room in the back lanes of one of the areas I needed to see. I walked in sceptically and saw Rinzin. His father came to meet me first.

We spoke about the jail system, the prisons. There was also an unverified report which later more than one person spoke of, that sometime around the end of 2007, a nun had immolated herself. Officially, the first recorded self-immolation is by a monk called Tapey on 27 February, 2009. He was from the very important Kirti Monastery.

What we need to remember here is that absolutely no agency can tell us how many people have committed self-immolation in Tibet accurately. We only know the names of those who did so in a crowded place and were somehow either photographed or recorded on video by someone around.

The question is not when did someone self-immolate oneself; the question is why.

What is the scale of violence against ordinary Tibetans that someone would feel the urge to burn themselves? Very often this was connected to the closing down of monasteries and the violence against great masters or the burning of scriptures. Entire monasteries have been shut by the Chinese authorities. Sometimes demolished completely if the monks and nuns did not adhere to what is called 're-education', which is a euphemism for making someone forcibly fall in line.

This evening, I met a lot of people who informed several aspects of *Pah-la*. Among others, there were two ex-prison guards and one person who still worked in a major prison.

The interviews and meetings continued, but it is here that Rinzin said the most extraordinary thing about Tibet. When someone said to him if he would like to meet His Holiness, pointing to how I was going to have an audience with him when I returned to India, he said he meets HH every day. Nobody is allowed to have his photo but everyone has him all the time.

How?, I asked. And this eight-year-old boy asked simply, 'If he is not here, then why is everyone saying every day that he is not here? There are people in my family who have gone away but everyone every day does not say it.' He said in Tibetan and his uncle translated.

The point he made was a big one. That in a way His Holiness had not left. In fact, the experience of having him around was real for the Tibetans, and the Chinese government knows this. It is not a prosaic real presence, like the government would have us believe. It is not that he calls people and they burn themselves. They know it is far more dangerous than that. That in Tibetan consciousness, he is present. Everywhere. It isn't magic, it is the fundamental belief of Tibetan society. That he is a living god. Like the capitalist world believes in infinite growth and the communists in China believe in the impending communist world-order, Tibetans believe that he is not a saint or a godman – he is god. That is what Rinzin had stumbled upon in his profound observation. That to say repeatedly that someone is not here is actually a way of remembering them every day. It was a way of taking his name and keeping his image alive.

I will never be able to forgive the people who starved Rinzin. I sometimes think that it is because of him that I put up with a lot that came later on.

He had been told that I make theatre. He said he loved theatre.

I had asked his uncle what theatre had Rinzin seen. His uncle had said that his family was a family of performers earlier. So they had carried their instruments and costumes to Lhasa. It was in his blood. He loved performances.

When people ask me, why I make theatre when its reach is so small, I often find myself thinking of Rinzin in that tea room in Lhasa.

'If he is not here, then why is everyone saying every day that he is not here?'

I can be in any art form of this world that allows me to hear that from an eight-year-old. Rinzin knew the theatre. He trusted me when he was told I make what he loves. To me that matters. That people believe theatre-makers.

In the day, Pallavi and I were visiting places according to our itinerary and both of us were collecting facts along the way. Pallavi was also clicking pictures which later on were my go-to resource to remember places. These were not photos that anyone could object to but were great placeholders for things to remember.

It was during one of these mornings that we went to Potala Palace. The Potala Palace is more beautiful than any picture of it can suggest. It is massive and is surrounded by mountains. Tibetans from various parts of Tibet come there every day and are lined up by soldiers. They are, I think, allowed to enter with a very nominal fee (or perhaps none) while tourists pay a higher fee to get in. We never meet each other. In fact, it is possible to travel all through Tibet without meeting a single Tibetan person who does not work for the Chinese government.

What is extraordinary is an extra room that the Chinese authorities have added just before entering the palace. It had old-style paintings with no cohesion to the actual old paintings inside, painted with new paint!

We were told that it was compulsory to go to this new 'old' room in order to enter.

This room had paintings that depicted the story of Princess Wencheng. The idea was simple. One had to see that Buddhism itself came in from Mainland China and then go ahead with the rest of the visit. Inside, we were to see one of the greatest wonders of art that I have ever seen and yet, according to the Chinese version, all that art stemmed from Princess Wencheng bringing Buddhism.

Potala Palace in its various corners has monks sitting and studying or chanting. They are also involved in several ritual practices. It is a masterclass on traditional performance. The immersive aspects of religious performance are present in their complete glory. It is astounding that the Chinese state objects to the mummification of the Dalai Lamas in the name of orthodoxy and unscientific thinking, but Mao Zedong's body is embalmed and preserved in Beijing. Beijing's most important tourist site in fact is this. People come from distant parts of China and queue up here to see his corpse. The same symbol there and here has different meanings.

There it is greatness and here it is superstition.

From the time we had arrived, I saw several houses with Chinese flags. In one of the interviews, I was told that actually this was a sign by and large that these were houses of Tibetans. It had become extremely important for Tibetans to show allegiance to the Chinese state post-2008.

Several interviews later, a few very important strands stood out.

First, that something unusual had happened in 2008. The scale of it was much larger than that in recent times.

Second, that there were several Chinese guards and prison workers who had resigned. These were people who were not reinforcement but had actually lived in Tibet for a few years. That there was a sort of moral Stockholm syndrome, and it is through these interviews I was able to see the real power of non-violence. That perhaps, in the end, freedom is going to mean something completely different in the next centuries than what we imagine it today. The nebulous nature of the boundaries of good and bad might extend new possibilities over the boundaries of national and ethnic differences. That the children of Han and Tibetans who grow up together might end up finding a radically different solution than the ones that exist. Non-violence provides that possibility. Whether it takes long or little time, it does not embed more violence into a violent world as it considers all acts and even thoughts of hatred violent. And if one spoke to prison guards and prison workers, one could see how the resolve of Tibetan non-violence had shaken them over the years when they knew perfectly well that even if their prisoners wanted, they could not turn violent. However, the fact that several prisoners worked hard at not hating those who beat them up was overwhelming for the prison guards. It is a change that I can see in the world because of this experience.

Third, that there definitely was an active sense among Tibetans that His Holiness was watching out for them in the world.

Fourth, that underneath all this, another kind of Tibetan struggle was emerging. And that non-violence could not forever be taken for granted.

And finally, that many people inside Tibet did not completely believe that His Holiness had opted for the middle path of autonomy from China over independence. This debate was alive as much inside as it is outside.

From Lhasa we went to Shigatse, the place from where many people used to start their walks across the Himalayas to come to

India. In Shigatse, one gets the eerie sense that it is a prison town. A town whose primary purpose is to make sure that no one can leave.

There were garrisons and soldiers everywhere.

By the time I am writing this, in 2021, it has become close to impossible to escape from Shigatse.

China has developed the ability to land war planes close to Sikkim in India on highways.

At the same time, I know that the independence movement inside Tibet is picking steam. It is combining with movements in other parts of China. The Uighurs were a big part of that kind of strong push against the central power-holding structure. I am unfortunately not surprised by the atrocities on them. The concentration camps and the forced re-education.

The model comes from Tibet.

From Shigatse, we left for Chengdu. We were there for a night and the next evening we flew out. I have never in my life felt so relieved at flying out of a place. It was not that I disliked China. There were several things about it that were rich and alive. And I met some of the most generous people who took great risks in Beijing and Lhasa to tell their stories. There was also incredible moral ambiguity and yet the sense that here was a place where a position, a belief, a name could decide on your life and death.

I had also met several people who betrayed all stereotypes about China and the Chinese state. People who had fought their superiors to save the lives of others. People who had protected others at the cost of their own jobs.

I had also met Tibetans who made me understand the importance and centrality of religion in their lives. Without their religion, they would not be able to remain non-violent at such a large scale for so long. They were the ones who were most disturbed by the attack on the school. They knew the difference between violence and crime.

As the plane left, I found myself thinking of the evening that Pallavi and I went to the Nangma bar in Lhasa. A Nangma bar is a Tibetan bar which has a huge hall, often with round tables, where Tibetan singers and actors perform their own music on stage. There are often projections of beautiful scenes, much like music videos, behind the singer.

It is a place that is seemingly outside of Chinese control. One could, from the look of it, do anything here. This was kept untouched by the authorities.

Except that later I got to know that this was not the case. Nangma bars were strategic tools by the government. Where people could meet and let out steam and yet everything was controlled by the government.

One of the most important things I have learnt about politics over the years is that it has gotten much smarter.

Lorca was killed by the dictatorship. Today's dictators would celebrate Lorca. They would construct a Lorca memorial. It would have merchandise. It would have a bar or a coffee shop where radical Lorca fans would gather and question the regime. Except they would be doing so in a place controlled by the government, done up in government-approved aesthetics and with government-approved food and drinks. Eventually, their discourse on Lorca will get thawed by the little benevolence and controlled freedom provided by the regime they are opposing. They would not only lose their freedom but also not realize that it is lost.

We are all in a giant Nangma bar in the world where we believe the songs and dances are ours. Where we believe that this site is untouched and that the government is not strong enough to take this from us. Except that this site will take away our ability to be radical. To demand freedom tonight.

This I thought, on that flight, was common to capitalism and modern Chinese communism.

However, I also thought of the wonderful people there, who waved at us in abundance as we entered. They kept sending us cans and cans of beer because we were Indians. They kept saying thank you in their own way.

As we left Chengdu, I knew we had done something extraordinary. A lot of it that will never be possible to write because of the well-being of others.

I was proud that both of us did it. We were out.

But I think the sense of being potentially seen and heard at all times never left me.

Tibet made me vigilant forever.

Even now if I see a shadow moving awkwardly to my side, something deep inside my body prepares me to move aside. Tibet and Kashmir have got internalized in me.

Fear is like that.

I cannot ever imagine what it must be like to live forever in that fear.

However, I could tell the stories that I did because of a pact I had made with the people in these places. Who told me their stories and said write. We believe in the theatre.

If not in so many words, then in gesture, change of breath and speed of talking, the moment they got to know I write plays.

Everyone had seen a play. In their context of their own culture, with its own dramaturgy.

They might have never read a book, but they had all sometime worn a costume and pretended to be someone else.

Their religions were filled with the same logic of performativity.

Maybe even core relationships like parenting, siblings, filial and maternal.

In the flight, we slept. I have never felt more tired getting out of a place.

V

India and HH the Dalai Lama

After returning to India, it took some time to collate all the material. There were several different strands. Notes from Dharamshala, McLeod Ganj, Bylakuppe in South India, Hong Kong, reports from Taiwan, from internet-based searches and from the trip to China and Tibet.

To me, the most essential parts of the research were set in the prison in Lhasa. It also served as a space where people from different walks of life could meet. Dramatically also, prison stories had been long of interest to me though I had never written one.

The first draft of *Pah-la* was written in a beautiful and picturesque guest house in Pune. FLAME (Foundation for Liberal Arts and Management Education) is a liberal-arts college set in the hills, and my friend and playwright Ashutosh Poddar, who teaches there, had invited me to teach a short scenography course. It was here that I wrote a draft entirely set in prison.

There are two ways of writing a Tibet play. One, to write from the perspective of those in exile, and the second, from those who are inside Tibet. The exile story and point of view are known to anyone who is interested in the subject because they are the only possible representatives of the culture. The important aspect I thought was to write the story from inside.

The moment we step into a culture, we are faced with many voices. Many doubts and aspirations of people that can find their ways into a play. At the same time, it is important to not lose sight of the bigger picture: What is the proposition of play on the subject that has not been offered before? How does it theorize the moral or philosophical problem at hand?

I had to go back to my original question and ask myself what would be the future of non-violence indeed.

To me, the answer was complicated. I think the answer *is* complicated. I think Tibet indeed is the last beacon of hope for non-violence. It is Buddhism that has kept it all together. Otherwise, there is no community in the world that faces this scale of oppression in today's time and that continues to identify itself primarily as a non-violent group.

At the same time, the Tibetan community in Tibet is non-violent also because of their religion. More specifically, in fact, because His Holiness the Dalai Lama has called for a non-violent approach. When I asked His Holiness himself later on in an interview if he thinks non-violence will last after him, he said, 'If people are non-violent, they have to be so from deep within. Not because the Dalai Lama asks them to be.'

There are already proto-revolutionary groups in Tibet which are forming solidarities with other movements. This does not mean that a large population is not non-violent. It means that other strands are emerging.

At FLAME, I set the play in a prison and it examined how difficult it was to remain non-violent in a place like Tibet.

For me, the most heroic thing about Tibetans was that they were ordinary people like the rest of us. They were not exotic beings who had some grand oriental scheme by which they never felt angry. They had all the usual emotions. The pushes and pulls.

However, they chose to remain non-violent in large numbers. Even in 2008, when there were instances of odd violence like the one in the school.

This version of *Pah-la* was then worked upon for many years and developed through workshops in multiple places. In London at the Royal Court. In Dharamshala with Lhakpa Tsering and Tibetan actors from his theatre community.

Like in my other plays, whatever was first-hand information was verified, and through various sources I tried to get permissions from everyone whose words, phrases or stories had been used in the play.

In one such workshop, Vicky Featherstone, the artistic director of Royal Court Theatre, suggested providing context to what brought these characters to prison. In fact, I think the point dramaturgically was more about the audience getting to see what life in Tibet is like.

I thought that was a brilliant suggestion and the play was divided into two acts. Till the fifth draft, it was set completely in the prison, but from the sixth onwards, it became about a nun called Deshar who lives in a monastery in Kham and is then forced to go through re-education in rural Tibet by Chinese soldiers. Without giving away too much of the plot, let us say that the second half is set in a prison in Lhasa.

The play was critical of the Chinese government and its policies, but it also questioned many positions of His Holiness the Dalai Lama. Particularly two positions.

The first is the choice to give up the quest for independence and the second, to not unequivocally stop the self-immolations in Tibet. I have to say that His Holiness commands an enormous power over Tibetans around the world. There are several historical instances in which a word from him has stopped a practice or started an institution.

With these questions on both sides, and hopefully without false equivalences, being completely aware that this work was more anthropological than experiential, I sent my draft to HH the Dalai Lama through his Foundation for Universal Responsibility.

Rajiv Mehrotra, who is the secretary of the trust, read the play and also signed me up for a three-day teaching of a central Buddhist text *Madhyamika* by His Holiness.

I was astonished that this was happening during the writing of a play. I had met commanders of police, hackers, people in exile, guides, revolutionaries, monks, nuns and a host of other people that I would never get to meet if I was not making this play.

Now here I was off to Delhi to meet His Holiness the XIV Dalai Lama.

VI

Meeting His Holiness

Let me say at the outset that I am not religious. I am an atheist. Militantly atheist. However, I have a deep interest in religion. Over the years, I have found myself extensively studying at least three religions for three different plays. Buddhism (particularly Tibetan Buddhism), early philosophical works and major scriptures in Hinduism and the history of Islam along with Quranic exegesis have been part of my work.

My interest lies in the fact that these religions are such a potent site of stories, metaphysics, social conditioning, psychological relief, philosophical debate, war, terror, orthodoxy and so much more. You name it and it is there. I cannot imagine another idea that still remains as strongly with us today as it was when it was invented, which is perhaps close to the time we accidentally discovered how to make a fire. In fact, I wouldn't be surprised if several beliefs in the supernatural even preceded the moment of the discovery of fire.

Once when Elyse Dodgson, the director of the international department at the Royal Court, and the person without whom I cannot imagine my writing, asked me sheepishly, 'Are you a Buddhist now?' I replied, 'No. I am a playwright.'

I have always believed that critically writing on religion and the practice of religion cannot coexist in the same person.

However, I still call His Holiness by this title.

This is because he is indeed the closest to the conception of what would be a noble god that I can imagine.

I attended two days of his complex classes on the *Madhyamika*. I had to study it before I reached, and it was extremely difficult for me to understand.

After two days of classes, the third morning, I was given ten minutes to meet him. He was in his room in a hotel in Delhi and his office had told him about the play. They had read it and briefed him.

I went to his door after the usual security checks. The door opened and there he was.

He had come to the door to take me inside.

He held my hand and we walked in. When we reached the sofa in his room, he waited.

I waited.

I couldn't even look at him. I knew he had been briefed about the play, and I had lines in there which criticize him brutally. But here he was, the Nobel-Prize winner, the god of all the Tibetans in the world, waiting for me to sit down before he would sit.

I somehow managed to sit, and for a moment he kept quietly looking at me. Then he buttoned the top button of my shirt and said, 'You'll catch a cold' and laughed an infectious laughter.

Interacting with His Holiness, one has to remind oneself that he is the god in the room. Otherwise, he can make the visitor feel like His Holiness has come to meet them.

His humility is not false humility that is often paraded as goodness. There is something completely different about His Holiness which is so genuinely accommodating and so present that one forgets the equation.

He said I have heard about your play. It is good. Ask me questions.

I started asking him several questions. Some extremely critical ones.

For instance, when I asked him if he did not feel that by turning non-violent, while Tibetan guerrilla forces like Chushi Gangdruk were still fighting in the front, he had betrayed them, he asked his staff to increase our time.

He shared not only his certainties but also his doubts and uncertainties, and at one point of time he said, 'Be critical of me. Tibetans think I am god, but you know I am not.' And then he laughed again.

There were many answers that I am not placing here. For I do not know if I have the right to do so. They were his private answers and I managed to have those as ambiguities of an evolved person in the play spread across characters.

He was extremely rational, and needless to say, his rhetorical skills are the greatest I have seen. To be a Dalai Lama, the Chosen, one goes through a programme in dialectics that is akin to an eighteen-year PhD!

To many of the questions I asked, which were moral questions, he replied with stories. He gave me a situation that was specific and contained a moral ambiguity. It was not the answer but the question itself that was the point of his answer.

I tried to use this technique in *Pah-la* as well. Especially since the premise of *Pah-la* was to do with prisons and polygraph machines,

I rewrote many sections with Deshar responding to the Chinese commander Deng with stories.

Our meeting extended to an hour.

By the end of it, he said to me that he was glad that young people like me were working on the Tibet story. He said that in the 1970s and 1980s there was a lot of interest in Tibet, but it seemed to have died out later especially among the young.

I asked him if I could ask him one last question.

He said yes.

I asked what he thought the world needed to remain non-violent and be peaceful. Why was the world a more violent place now although we had more of everything?

He said,

> When we find a camera that can show us the thief's intention and not just the action, we will then truly be in a position to empathize and not punish. All cameras are only catching the thief now and that is why every government is making more borders, adding more surveillance and yet there is more violence. The day we can know the intention of the thief and empathize with it, that day I will believe that we have advanced technologically.

I got up awkwardly to leave since I did not know what was the gesture to leave. I did not want to do anything meaningless, irreverent or religious. At the same time, I was immensely moved.

He solved this problem too.

He touched my head and held my face. He said, 'Take care of yourself.'

I said yes. Thank you, your Holiness.

I left that room with one of the greatest experiences of my life. Something I will cherish forever.

All the hardships and risks I thought were justified.

Pah-la has had thirteen drafts. Now, the fourteenth is getting translated to Tibetan and will open in 2022 in Tibetan language.

The drafts have gone through many changes. Several layers of censorship have been fought against. It has taught me several deep aspects of storytelling.

It has also taught me what it means to tell stories that belong to other people.

However, the journey of writing *Pah-la* to a degree was over. After meeting His Holiness, I felt enriched, excited and deeply rewarded for being a theatre-maker.

In later years, the making of this work was followed by death threats, attempts to buy out the play, stop it through coercion and once, a direct physical attack on me. I understood then what His Holiness meant by saying, 'Take care of yourself.'

Pah-la has easily been one of the greatest experiences for me. I still have friends in Tibet whose families and friends in exile keep in touch with. I learnt enormously about the world and the question I had set out with.

Pallavi says she remembers a lot about this journey. I believe it must have been a significant experience for her too.

Elyse unfortunately died before *Pah-la* opened. I miss her every day of my writing life. I wish I could have shown her this play.

Rinzin too was not alive when it opened.

However, I hope as the Tibetan production travels hereon to different parts of the world, that the Tibet story travels. There are several new Tibetan writers coming to the fore.

In time, I am sure, the Tibet story will unravel in many complex ways and several Tibetans will be telling that story to the world.

For me, *Pah-la* was a purely selfish act. A storyteller's undying urge to chase a question. Several people of several nationalities helped me chase that question.

There were days of the utmost high to days of utter despair.

In the end, I can only thank the world for giving me this opportunity to tell this story. And for common people to believe in the theatre.

7

Devising in the Tibetan Transit School

Dharamshala. India. Tibetan Transit School.

Dharamshala and McLeod Ganj are twin cities in the state of Himachal Pradesh in India. Himachal Pradesh is home to the Himalayas, the great mountain range separating the plains of the Indian subcontinent from the high Tibetan Plateau. The state is one of the most significantly populated pockets in the mountain range and marked with wide valleys, imposing snow-capped mountains, crystalline lakes and gushing meltwater rivers. Owing to its agreeable mountain climate and scenic setting, Shimla, the capital of Himachal Pradesh, became the summer capital of the British Raj. The retreat for the white rulers, famous for its balls, parties and marriage alliances.

There are other picturesque towns in Himachal Pradesh, and among these most unique places are these twin cities. For they are home to His Holiness the 14th Dalai Lama, Tenzin Gyatso. His residence and monastery are here, as is also the Parliament of the Tibetan Government in Exile and the Central Tibetan Administration (CTA). Since his dramatic escape from China after the Tibet Uprising in 1959, His Holiness has made India his home. Since then, Tibetans have come in large numbers from Tibet to meet him. To stay, to continue their education in Tibetan schools, to move into the world outside India and live their lives as both monastic and non-monastic people.

The Chinese persecution in Tibet started in the time of Mao Tse-tung himself, although initially he kept a wait-and-watch policy, which eventually turned to an all-out annexation and occupation of Tibet. What has followed since is an attack on Tibetan culture, its language and way of life. Since His Holiness left Tibet, the journey from Tibet to India via Nepal has been considered one of the most treacherous and epic journeys in modern times. Till about 2008–9, people were still escaping from Tibet in small groups, often with a guide who would take them on a journey across the mountains on foot, a treacherous trek over soaring peaks from where the Everest would be visible. Moreover, this journey had to be mostly made at night using very little light in order to avoid being caught by Chinese patrols. In the day, they would hide and rest in crevices in the mountains, and at night, the journey would begin again. The odds were heavily stacked against them. Even among the parties that did make it to the other side of the Himalayas, rarely did all the travellers survive the trek. But despite these terrifying odds, several Tibetan families sent their young ones on this journey out of fear that they had no future in Tibet.

For Tibetans inside Tibet, this future does not necessarily mean a move to something material. I interviewed many Tibetans who escaped to India during the research of my play *Pah-la*. Although many Tibetans – as per my interviews – suggested that they left Tibet because they feared unequal opportunities for themselves, the reason they left in most cases was for their language, religion and culture.

Classical Tibetan language is one of the oldest classical languages of the world. This extraordinarily complex language has different grammar principles across different periods of its existence, and it contains some of the world's richest sources of Buddhist philosophy and dialectic. It should also be noted that modern Tibetan language also has at least three major strands: Lhasa, Khams and Amdo. While the former two have some similarities, I am told that Amdo Tibetan is very different from the two. This Tibetic language set is extremely complex, unlike the primitivism that Chinese government accuses it of in order to introduce the rampant study and use of Mandarin.

The Chinese crackdown on this language and religion has led to all major schools of Tibetan Buddhism setting up their main centres in India, with their greatest masters moving out, very often carrying their precious scriptures with them so that they do not get destroyed. I found quite clearly from the interviews that the preservation of knowledge in Tibetan language was one of the key motivators for this journey.

In fact, the first institution that His Holiness had set up in India was the Tibetan Institute of Performing Arts (TIPA) in Dharamshala. Even today, an enormous amount of Tibetan language, culture and knowledge is held in the wide range of performance traditions in the Tibetan milieu that include opera, dramatic plays, live music, puppetry, poetry and more recently, cinema. In fact, many cultural contests are fought by the Chinese government by changing the narratives of Tibetan performances inside Tibet.

Two major institutions set up by His Holiness are Tibetan Children's Villages (TCV) and Tibetan Transit School (TTS), now renamed as Sherab Gatsel Lobling School. The former provides education and stay to several children who do not have parents and to refugee children of Tibetans who make this journey, while the latter provides stay and an integration programme for young adults running from three to five years.

In 2014, I had the opportunity to spend some days at Tibetan Transit School, conducting a theatre workshop along with the director of Tibet Theatre, Lhakpa Tsering, towards the casting and development of *Pah-la*. I was told before I went in that we were essentially going to work with non-actors. Some of them had never performed at all, and most had definitely never performed in the context of what is generally considered to be modern dramatic theatre. However, many of them had indeed been part of ritual performances on religious or commemorative occasions.

Lhakpa and I went into the workshop and started with a simple introduction. The participants, ranging from the age of eighteen to thirty, sat in a circle with us.

Over the several interviews I had already conducted, I had observed that Tibetans often do not speak about their trauma, challenges and journey early on. They obviously understand the importance of telling their story to the world, but at the same time, they are also people who in their day-to-day lives more often than not focus on Buddhist principles of focusing on the positives rather than dwelling on the pain and frustrations. I had seen them open up on the trauma only after several meetings and interviews, by which time they would be absolutely raring to tell every detail of their journey so that nothing is missed in the telling.

However, we were in the space of theatre now.

After we sat in a circle, Lhakpa introduced me, and then soon after, we were up on our feet walking through the space and doing simple theatre warm-ups through which we were introducing ourselves. Some of the participants spoke in English, some in Hindi; both languages accessible to me. But there were many who spoke in Tibetan and Lhakpa translated them for me.

As the introductions went on, I noted that the room was filled with men and women who had arrived here the hard way: by walking across the Himalayas.

We moved from these introductions to simple improvisations. Working with several different communities, I have noticed that it is here in these improvisations that people begin to reveal first how much is their own desire to 'play' and then, implicitly, what dramaturgy does their culture hold.

In most dramaturgical frameworks, there is a focus on the 'event' as a building block of constructing a dramatic narrative. My own classes as a playwriting instructor often begin with a module on writing a scene around a place and an event. I remember this also being the first 'provocation' in London International School of Performing Arts (LISPA), the Lecoq-based drama school I attended. We see this belief in the event as the fundamental building block in writing rooms around the world. And I have encountered this notion repeatedly across several dramaturgical discussions across theatres in many countries. A perpetual reiteration of the belief that an event will trigger action and that action elaborated in time is what ultimately drama is.

This parameter of looking out for events and actions is such an axiom that, more often than not, world over dramaturgical practices distinguish between good and bad drafts based on this principle, irrespective of where the play is coming from or which society it represents. New forms of art have been created over the years to respond to this crisis of event and action; durational performance art and site-specific installation are testament to it. However, in rooms buzzing with dramaturgical decisions on dramatic narrative plays, this hegemony of event and action is very hard to escape.

However, in that room of the workshops, and later on when I was in Tibet and Sikkim (a state in Northeast India that is another site of Tibetan practice), it became evident to me that the Tibetan dramatic oeuvre is not about the event.

Something of course happens in Lhamo Opera, or in the performance at the monasteries, but not unlike – I suppose – in Noh theatre of Japan, the thing that is happening is not the core of the performance. The action is not keeping track of time as it does in Aristotelian structures. For instance, every scene in *Antigone* is telling us that the burial is delayed, and hence, time is at premium and that something must be done soon.

In fact, a significant canon of Western dramatic literature is built on this idea of compression of time. We talk about deviations in Beckett or Ionesco, but a closer look shows us that inside these deviations the sense of compression of time remains. *Waiting for Godot* is known to be a play where 'nothing happens', but it is still full of *micro*-events. Every page has details of quarrels and objectives. The waiting is long because the objectives are so many.

In contrast, let us consider a very popular Tibetan play, *The Tale of Milarepa*. Milarepa was a practitioner of Tibetan Buddhism in the fifteenth century. He was a sorcerer and a murderer as a young man in the story, who then turned to the noble path. The tale is full of events, but when we watch a performance of it, it is evident that the events are not foregrounded. What is foregrounded are the reflections. The pauses and the working of the mind of Milarepa, who has to struggle to break his habits, thoughts and negative feelings in order to come out on the other side as a changed individual. Hence, this dramaturgy is significantly different from that of, say, *Antigone* or *Oedipus Rex*.

That day at the Tibetan Transit School, as Lhakpa and I worked with the participants on their improvisations, we faced a huge conflict. Lhakpa was prompting them to expand, whereas I was giving them situations where my expectation as a facilitator was to see how the compression of time would affect the telling of their stories.

Every human being I have ever seen in a rehearsal room, whether they think of themselves as performers or not, essentially comes from a theatre culture. This culture is visible not only in the design, style of performance, music and the content of stories but also in the way one enters the stage and the way one stands. In several drama schools around the world, actors are told to 'take space'. However, in many cultures like the one we were in, 'taking space' is fundamentally a concept that the culture theologically works against. One enters the stage in a Tibetan ritual performance like

The Tale of Milarepa to make visible the journey from the conscious to the subconscious, and to view the sameness in good and evil ('awareness of sameness' being one of the five Buddhist wisdoms manifested in a purified mind) and not to view victory of one over another. Tibetan culture is not a culture of contest. Their plays have good and evil, but they are not cast as heroes and villains, granted with nuances and deep motivations, and who argue their unchangeable positions. They are actually not representing real people in that dramatic culture. The contest is with oneself and not dialectically arranged between opposing people.

Within our improvisations, there were of course some moments in which some actors were more present than others, some in which some were more forthcoming and adventurous than others, but I kept having a nagging feeling that there was something I was asking them to do that was not the point of what they intrinsically thought theatre was.

One learns theatre, I believe, at home. Drama schools shape the ability to perform and structure ideas and emotions in time. However, usually the first live performances one sees are at home while play-acting as a child and, in many cases, the neighbourhood religious play in several cultures. These could be the *Ramlila*, Nativity plays, plays in the monastery or the *Ta'zieh* – but in my understanding, dramatic purpose is etched into a person at this stage. And for those who go on to become theatre artists, their life's work thereon is to find a way of recreating that feeling, that aesthetic and that sense of magic.

So many theatre festivals and venues around the world struggle so hard to programme their international work with a deep dramaturgical understanding because they often have no idea what is the first theatre that this practitioner has seen. So, while the practitioner's theatre might travel, the sociocultural context it was made and seen in is usually lost and not understood in its own terms. And hence, while theatres are very happy to commission international artists to become native informants in anthropological terms, to tell them something about the world, they end up relying exclusively on their own artists to tell them something about love, fear, anger and other core emotions.

In a Tibetan performance, even after so many years of political struggle, one would very rarely find a scene of the Brechtian kind, where compression of time and alienation of character coexist at the same time. In Tibetan performances, the elaboration of pain and joy is meant to elaborate the politics.

I was beginning to understand some of my own limitations as the writer of *Pah-la* at this stage. That if done properly, this has to be a play not about events but about the inner workings of the people that are in fact not converted to action.

In the break, we continued to chat and I asked a young woman what had prompted her to take the workshop. She told me she wanted to tell her story and reflect on it. I asked her which story would that be and she replied, 'The walk. About how I came here.'

I asked her if she thinks people would be comfortable doing improvisations around that theme and she said most of them would.

We then asked the actors if they would like to improvise around the theme of the travel, and everyone immediately agreed. I was surprised because I had found in my interviews that it is not the first thing that Tibetans want to talk about, and one must of course respect that. It must be such a traumatic experience.

However, here they were. Perhaps, still not wanting to speak about it but willing and wanting to perform it again. This time in the safety of this rehearsal room. To live it once more in a manner that one could actually respond to it. At one level, it is a purely aesthetic desire to make a play, and at another, as with many aesthetic desires, its roots lie deep within our own experience. Very often about things that have had a deep impact on us but which we do not know how to access.

The next day, we gathered again and I told the actors we would begin with the first part, which was about leaving home. We would work in groups of four or five and, after discussion, recreate a scene which could be completely fictional but drawing from the experience of all the participants in each group.

In an hour and half, we sat down in a large hall with a big picture of His Holiness hanging from the wall, where they started to present in groups some of the most riveting scenes I have ever seen in theatre. Despite being so-called 'non-actors', they performed the scenes with the kind of precision and elaboration that most professionals would struggle to achieve. The experience was not only lived but by now, in the time between arriving in India and this workshop, it was also something they wanted to live again. Most Tibetans who left home have never spoken to their families again. It is through great strife and luck that few have managed to find a way of calling home, through some kind of network that allows them to speak to their parents once in a while. I have known of people who left Tibet in the 1980s and spoke to their parents for the first time in 2010.

Here was a group of Tibetans performing that scene of leaving home. In one of the scenes, there was a young girl who looked at her grandparents one last time and then leaves. The focus was again not on the event, as she took her time to explore the house, the little bag she was going to take with her and how she just looked at their sleeping figures before leaving. There was nothing else in terms of events. No one cried, no goodbyes, for she had not told them she was leaving – but it was all done with great emotion and clarity.

There was one scene in which a young man gets out of prison and immediately leaves for Shigatse, the place from where he was to start his walk again. Almost no one I interviewed during the many years of this work had made it out of Tibet in one attempt. More often than not, they were arrested and released with a warning the first time. The second time would be more severe, and if one were caught the third time, I was told over and over again that the consequences would be unimaginable.

This improvisation on leaving home made me later reflect on how fundamental and universal the theme of leaving home is. *Iliad*, *Ramayana*, *Mahabharata*, *Odyssey*. In fact, the Islamic calendar starts not with the Prophet's (PBUH) birth but the Hijri, that is, when he had to leave Mecca for Medina. This moment of leaving home, which is already such a fundamentally significant moment for all, becomes even more significant for young Tibetans.

In one improvisation, a group presented a person's dilemma about whether they should carry a picture of their parents or not. If they did not, they would perhaps forget their faces. But on the other hand, if they did, the parents were absolutely certain to get into trouble if the young person was caught by the authorities while crossing the mountains.

We wrapped the day's exercises, deciding we would resume with the exercises the next day and get back to the second part of this improvisation of leaving home, in which they would improvise around the actual journey.

Lhakpa and I parted ways in the evening, and I met my friend Dawa who is a monk. Dawa had come to McLeod Ganj in the summer for some special classes on certain aspects of Tibetan

Buddhism. He is a monk of the Gelupa sect, the same as His Holiness.

Dawa and I have shared a very special bond. We would meet a few times a week on the terrace of a hotel and discuss Buddhist philosophy, among other things. I taught him English in the day, and he taught me ideas far more complex in the evening. Dawa had been born in Tibet himself and had walked with his sister to India. Then he studied in TCV, after which he felt his calling was to be a monk, and hence, took up monastic life. He is a great scholar, already quite well known in monastic circles. His debates are especially fascinating. We debated every evening over the various problems he brought to our table, where we had tea together. He always drank lemon tea and I had the strongest possible Assam tea, and this was just the beginning of our differences.

We always started our discussion by sharing details of our day and to my surprise, he told me that he too loved to act when I told him of the workshop I was conducting with Lhakpa.

Lhakpa himself is quite well known and is quite a young hero of the Tibetan revolution. He had famously immolated himself in front of the Taj Hotel in Mumbai when the Chinese Premiere, Hu Jintao, was visiting India in 2006. He had burnt his legs and stomach while shouting slogans of 'Free Tibet', before the security forces saved him. I have never gotten used to his courage even after knowing him for so many years. It is not surprising that he is the head of what is perhaps the first Tibetan theatre group in exile called Tibet Theatre.

Dawa and I discussed acting that day, and he told me about all the plays he had acted in during many functions in school. He laughed and told me, 'In monastic life, we have to act a lot. Every day, we debate with our fellow students, and sometimes we act a bit angrier at the argument than we really are.'

Like most monks I met in my years of work with the Tibetan community, Dawa has both an incredible intellect and a wicked sense of humour.

He told me that if I were to make a play on Tibetans, it should not be focused on monks alone, for that is what mostly happens. He was clear that the next day would be even more alarming for me because we would cover the actual journey. He had already told me about his experience and I asked him if it would be hard for him to recreate it if he had to as an actor.

He said, 'No. It is an experience. Like any other experience. Like you and I are sitting here and drinking tea. I could revisit it just to see if I am now less angry about it.'

As always, he reminded me of something fundamental. That I was in a culture where emotion was not being brushed under the carpet, and yet, the 'event' was not its fundamental association. That I was in a culture where equanimity, and not avoidance, is the norm and its most active political stance.

The next day, we started by talking about the journey. What were the different routes, the different kinds of guides on the way, the different circumstances in which people left and who could leave with some family members(s) and who had to leave alone. After this, the participants did a series of improvisations, with Lhakpa and me often dipping in.

In my theatre life, I have seen two kinds of challenges emerge during such improvisations. Either the creators sit and talk far too long, thereby leaving very little time for the actual rehearsal of the piece. Or they jump in too soon and begin doing a series of physical interpretations without being clear about what exactly are they interpreting. However, in this case, it was very precise. They had made these journeys and suddenly – unlike in the interviews – they were not only particularly expressive but also full of details. They were not trained actors but the climb and the walk were still in their bodies. Some of them had come here so recently that they still had frost bite on their feet. One of the participants had lost two of his fingers on the feet during the crossing.

Watching them make that work – as Lhakpa and I discussed later – two thoughts crossed our minds. First, they were so precise and expressive that there would be no actor who could recreate their journey as detailed as it was etched in their own memories. Second, it was evident that if this were to be taken into a rehearsal process, chances would be that they would not be able to recreate this. That since they were not trained actors, the rehearsals would most likely lose the vitality of these first improvisations drawn from their experience. This is one of the greatest challenges in the artifice of acting. It is real but it is life twice removed, as the performance theorist Richard Schechner says. A performance is ultimately a representation of a rehearsal which itself is a representation of reality.

However, in the Transit School, the bridge from reality to artifice seemed effortless. We saw scenes of falling, climbing, being caught by Chinese police and the most heart-breaking of them all where a group enacted a moment when they had to choose whether to leave an old man behind and carry on to save the rest of the lives, or to try to carry him on their backs since he could no longer continue on his own.

I do not think I have ever been in a workshop in which what had happened to the actors had been this intense. And yet, the artifice of the mode of their presentation of that experience, in this case through scenic improvisation, seemed that simple for them. They improvised with utmost commitment, thereby bringing to the work an extremely high degree of integrity. Nothing was done with the intent to impress anyone. Not an extra tug of emotion and not a single insecure forced moment of comic relief.

And in many drama classes around the world, I had seen situations where the group presenting was giving complete attention to their performance in order to receive a positive assessment from the teachers, while the group watching was still murmuring among itself about their own nearing presentation. Over here, all performances were watched rapt, and people who had so clinically performed their own improvisations cried as they saw stories of others who went through what they went through too.

Once we finished this, we gave each other feedback. Three of the participants had trained in other forms of art. If I remember correctly, one was a singer and the other two had trained in dance. They had borrowed heavily from their practices and had created moments of truth beyond anything I could have ever hoped to glimpse through in the interviews I had conducted.

We stayed with these improvisations for two days. Looking at them, recreating them and trying to see if there was a narrative we could create by placing some of the improvisations next to each other.

This journey is perhaps one of the most profound journeys of modern times. A mother leaves with her eight-month-old child to walk across some of the highest peaks in the world while escaping one of the world's most organized and brutal armies. And she does this to meet her god. His Holiness the Dalai Lama. To see him once and to get her child blessed by him.

In Tibet, this is not superstition. This is the way of life. Very often, I have found people looking down upon this and comparing this action to going on some kind of superstitious pilgrimage. What we must understand is that Tibetans do not walk across mountains to go for pilgrimage. They are walking away from a way of life that destroys the bedrock of their civilization, towards a refuge where their God is a refugee.

This is a very important idea to understand to make any theatre about Tibet. An idea that I believe was unpacked for me during this workshop. The equivalent of this journey is not that of Christians going to the Vatican or Muslims to Mecca or Hindus to Kailash Mansarovar. The equivalent is of people fleeing the ISIS to escape being stripped of every marker of their rights, desires and fundamental way of life. His Holiness is neither their saint nor their site of pilgrimage. He is, in fact, their God.

Our last day at the workshop was about to begin. Lhakpa and I walked down the hill from the main road to our rehearsal hall, wondering where we would go from what we had just seen. On arriving there, we told them we were now going to do an improvisation about going back to Tibet. The day when you return.

We were initially met with silence. This was not a scenario they had been in. In fact, for most of them it was a scenario unlikely to ever appear in their life, although every day they wished it would.

We were waiting to see what happens in the room as we heard some nervous laughter, some uncomfortable grunts when one of them asked, 'Are we going back to Tibet under China or to Free Tibet?'

'Free, of course. Free Tibet', both of us immediately replied.

They were up in no time. With much greater enthusiasm than even the previous days. There was no doubt at all about playing this scenario. This was something that had not happened in reality but had perhaps been played in their minds several times.

They worked for half a day on their own with some inputs from Lhakpa and me. In the afternoon, we sat down again to see the presentations.

With every improvisation, the audience cheered at every step. The moment a person entered the stage, people cheered because they had entered and set foot on Free Tibet.

A girl cried on just walking on to the stage. She then went on to perform a scene in which she goes back to her grandparents' room and meets them after several years.

A young man performed a scenario where he finally places the Dalai Lama's photograph on the wall of his house, and has to no longer keep it hidden in a trunk as he would have to under the Chinese occupation where it is illegal to carry the Dalai Lama's photograph.

There was a version in which a brother and sister both return and meet their father alone because their mother had died while they were away. In real life, they had gotten to know of their mother's death quite recently.

At the end of the workshop, we asked the participants what they thought of the workshop, and they unanimously agreed that the last improvisation was their favourite. Some said that they could do that one every day.

This particular day's impression on me is one of the factors that made me later decide that this is more than one play. Currently, I think it's a trilogy in which the first part is *Pah-la*, set in Tibet in 2008 during the Lhasa Uprising. The second part will be set in the mountains and is the chronicle of this journey. And the third will be about a young boy or a girl who lives in exile and washes dishes in a hotel. It is about a god, in exile. The second and third are yet to be worked upon.

As we prepare the ground for the Tibetan production of *Pah-la*, I often hear from several people that Tibetans are not professional actors. To this, my only response is that Tibetans are the best professional actors in their language.

By this, I do mean not only spoken language but also dramatic language.

Sometimes in our quest of internationalism and making it accessible to everyone (to the West really), we forget that in reality there is no empty space.

No such thing exists on which an actor can walk in and walk out which is empty. Every space in this world is laden with meaning and context.

What we call dramatic performance – truth, muscle memory, biomechanics and so on – all is connected to the meaning of a particular space. We change the space and the artifice changes.

We did not have sets, lights, costumes in the workshop, and most definitely we did not have an empty space.

To understand and appreciate Tibetan performers on stage, it is important that theatre clarifies the context, the philosophical dimensions, the meanings of their space. Inside which repetition is not only difficult but perhaps even undesirable.

It could well be that some people in this world make theatre for primarily two most important things to them. To be able to remember those they might never meet again. And to be able to go to a place whose flag, symbols, language, poetry and freedom are to be fought for. One improvisation at a time.

8

Reading George C. Wolfe's *The Coloured Museum* in a New York subway

I

In 2012, I travelled to New York City to attend the Lincoln Centre Directors Lab. This laboratory has been made possible by the tireless efforts of Anne Cattaneo, head-dramaturg at Lincoln Centre, and it used to bring together nearly seventy directors from across the world. Over a month of staying and working together, these directors picked up the most extraordinary skills and formed an invaluable community. Ten years on, I still owe this lab many of my closest friendships in theatre and even some very fruitful collaborations thereon. The lab in New York shut down post-pandemic in 2022. There are conversations to have other versions of this around the world, a Mediterranean lab already being present with directors from around the region.

I was attending the lab with my friend and colleague from India, Sandeep Shikhar. It was our first trip to the United States, and even now it amuses me how we arrived in New York at its peak summer with our suitcases full of winter-wear! We had seen the city only in the movies, and it was always snowing in them! We had arrived expecting a snow-trimmed city, posh and beautifully lit. Just like Hollywood had shown us. This was not our first travel abroad, but that picture-perfect image of New York, set to the lilting score of

Simon & Garfunkel, had been so strongly planted in us that we had absolutely no reason or agency to doubt it.

And so, when we landed there and made our way out of the airport, it was a massive surprise to say the least. The city looked old, run-down and was very hot. In more ways than one, it reminded me of Calcutta. And that too the really old parts.

I went to Brooklyn to live with a friend from the drama school I attended in London, while Sandeep stayed at the dorms of the Juilliard School. The next day, my friend took us around Brooklyn and we ended the evening on the terrace of a Brooklyn apartment, sitting and drinking with other theatre-makers, discussing till late what we cared about and what theatre meant to us and what it took in our respective cities to make the work one really wants to make. A conversation common and essential to theatre people around the world.

After a couple of days, I started going to the lab at the Lincoln Centre. While on the one hand the lab was extremely invigorating and exciting, on the other, the city made absolutely no sense to me. It was nothing like what had been promised to me by countless Hollywood films. I was getting exhausted by its heat, still could not figure out its subway and felt overwhelmed by its size and pace.

Just like in the process of making theatre, I do not like cities that are too fast. I struggle in Bombay even now, and New York is Bombay magnified many times over. Also, I have never understood why exactly does a fast city need to be fast. I have never seen a city known for its speed be any more productive than a city that isn't. 'Rush', I think, is an excuse to explain the demise of quality of life.

Having said this, I had been to enough cities to know that there was something mysterious about this city. Something driving it that was invisible to me. I realized that a city of this size and variety could not possibly be this homogenous, but my experience of it was limited to my commute between Brooklyn and Lincoln Centre.

During this time, I was getting more and more fascinated by the lives of Black people in Brooklyn. Growing up in Delhi in the mid-1980s, some of my first friends were Africans since my school had many students from Nigeria, Kenya and Uganda. However, I had no experience of African American culture other than a wonderful African American friend from the drama school in London.

With Brooklyn, I could already tell that it was something quite different. It had a different energy. A life I had not seen anywhere else in the world. Every day, I used to see an old Black lady standing on the way to the subway station, inviting people to come to her church. And I kept telling myself that I would take up that offer some day, for I believe religious places offer a deep insight into the culture of a place.

But for days I kept going back and forth on that subway and was beginning to feel frustrated by this city. By its ephemeral quality. And by my own incapability to still accept that New York was nothing like the city I had seen in *Home Alone*!

Then one day, on my morning commute to Lincoln Centre, I was changing sim cards on my phone, from my New York one to the India one in order to call home, when someone complained against me on suspicion. I am still not quite sure what that suspicion was, but I was asked to step out by cops after a few stops and was told that I had been reported. They wanted to check my bag and so on. I messaged Lincoln Centre that I would be late due to this, and when the matter was sorted out, the cops apologized saying it was the Olympic season and so they were on high alert.

The Olympics were in London. This was 2012.

In the coming days, the cops called me twice more to check where I was, and this stopped only after Lincoln Centre directly called the Mayor's office to stop the harassment. I told them it was not an issue. I had seen police harassment in India and had known it to be far worse. I was just not expecting to walk into it in New York. However, this experience left me even more confused. That such an incident could happen in a city that had looked so hugely cosmopolitan caught me by surprise.

I also attributed this incident to the way I looked. At that time, I was keeping a slight beard. I am of course a brown-skinned man, and I could be from many places if one takes a look at me. On top of that, I was conducting apparently the heinous crime of changing a sim card. While in drama school in London, I had been offered thrice bit roles in films. All three times, I was to play a terrorist. Needless to say, I did not take any of those offers.

During this time of confusion, the African American playwright George C. Wolfe came to the lab for a master class. He completely lit it up. He was funny, sensitive, poignant and deeply political. He spoke about his work and asked us about ours. While he spoke of America, he spoke invariably about race.

At the lab, play texts used to be kept on a table and we could pick up whichever script we wanted and return it in a couple of days after reading it. I picked up a copy of Wolfe's *The Coloured Museum* and carried it to the subway that night. I took the train from Lincoln Centre and took out the play to read. As the train moved from Manhattan towards Brooklyn, the world around me soon started to change colour. A lot of white people got down in Manhattan, and although many still remained when we entered Brooklyn, the train had definitely tilted its demographics towards people of colour. *The Coloured Museum* was coming alive in front of me.

This brilliant play is a farce shaped as series of vignettes that begin with the arrival of a slave ship called *Celebrity Slaveship*, and from then on, vignette after vignette explores the diversity of Black lives in America. From the historical shackling of slaves to the present-day irony of families forced to adopt white-upper-class manners in order to belong. With vignettes ranging from a monologue by a Black soldier returning from war to the stereotypical depiction of Black families on television soaps, the play plants its brutal gaze on the cost of oppression. At how deeply racism affects the Black community in America. And it does so not by showing the pain but rather the many masks and tropes that are needed to conceal it. It is a jab at the conscience of America by laying bare the defence mechanisms of its Black people.

Theatre had come to my defence again. Sitting on the subway, the next few days I read this play over and over again, shuttling back and forth between Brooklyn and Manhattan. Depending on the direction I was taking, it read differently; some vignettes seeming more real than others. It was as if history had comfortably placed itself not in a circle or in forward-moving time but in a bidirectional train. Suddenly, a play had given me an entry to the city. A method I truly love and strongly recommend: of reading plays about specific cultures while travelling through its towns and cities.

II

Every city is a site of performance. Be it a bus-trip around Delhi or the London Underground or the New York subway, all present to us the scenography of urban civilization. When we take a routine route, not being surprised by anything but absorbing the monotony of infinitesimally small changes that appear along, it reveals to us something deeper not only about the route but also about our society.

The Japanese philosopher Nishida used to walk the same route every day from his house to Kyoto University, where he founded the Kyoto School of Philosophy that synergized and contextualized Eastern and Western philosophy significantly for each other. This walk was taken in total silence, and when he would arrive at the university, he would conduct the most passionate classes. It is now famously called 'The Philosopher's Walk' because it is said that it was in these walks that he did a lot of his thinking, being deeply aware and observant of his surroundings.

Similarly, in bus- and train-routes, we see the everyday. The everyday that has the shape of the great joys, sorrows, frustrations and fault-lines of our society. We are at an intimate distance to others and yet not intruding. The space creates the opportunity to be an observer of life that is not a snapshot but a collage of images and sounds.

Journeys have often been part of theatre. Many ritual theatre performances around the world assume travel to the site to be a part of the performance. Hence, in these traditions, there are particular rituals of leaving home, songs for the journey, particular sites where particular actions happen and performances of meetings before the actual event of the play happens at a given site.

In India, the *Ramlila* of Ramnagar (a town in northern India) is one such fascinating performance. It lasts over several nights and during this time the small town of Ramnagar, itself part of a larger town called Ayodhya, gets converted to the site of *Ramayana*. Audiences come from all over the country, including tourists and academics from all parts of the world. They are given maps detailing which site in Ramnagar is going to play which episode of the epic. They follow the story of Rama as he is born in the king's palace (the Maharaja of Ramnagar is the official host) and then travel with him across the town as he travels from Ayodhya to the forest of Kishkinda, and from there to Lanka to fight Ravana, and finally returns to the palace at the end of the *Ramlila*. Hence, in that period, the town transforms into a sacred geography from a strictly cartographic one. Similarly, in Orissa, an eastern state of India, another *Ramlila* travels across villages, where the villagers of each passing village become part of Rama's entourage who travel to the next village.

The German documentary theatre company Rimini Protokoll uses a similar idea in its brilliant *Remote X* series, which are performances set in different cities of the world. The audiences gather in small groups and are given headphones along with a route map. As they travel through the city, the recording gives them a text of the city they are navigating. The text displaces what people might usually see about a site. It makes the mundane extraordinary and gives context to the extraordinary.

And so, the world over, there are many versions of such travelling theatre which contextualizes and de-contextualizes a space. Ranging from what we call traditional ritual theatre to what is termed postmodern and non-narrative work.

However, in my view, journeys are theatrical in themselves. Especially journeys within a city with no particular agenda. And especially while reading a text.

When we run a playwriting or direction class in India, an assignment that I often give to the students is to travel together in trains to three different heritage sites in the country whose art and aesthetics have developed under very different motivations. One site might have been built to display the grandeur of a kingdom to the largest possible audience, another site might be caves tucked far away from public gaze with beautiful Buddhist paintings used for meditation and the third could be a ritual community site that has over the centuries developed into a wonderful site of art. During this trip, students are to keep a journal about what they see from the train. How the aesthetics change with land and caste in India. It takes about ten to fifteen days to complete this journey. And many students have told me that this assignment taught them more about aesthetics than anything else they might have learnt in the classroom.

Journeys like these allow us to observe and reflect at the same time. And a journey through uncurated territory makes us the curators.

Society has curated itself through several invisible forces. Too many environmental, sociological, political, religious and psychological factors have come together over centuries and millennia to shape the art and aesthetics of the world around us. This pattern is hidden in an exquisite tapestry of theme, motivation and the course of history. And plays often try to capture not a moment but a general sense of the truth about this tapestry. This is why I think they read best when travelling through the landscape where this tapestry might be present.

In my university days in Delhi, I regularly took a particular bus called Mudrika, which means 'to go around'. This bus went around Delhi along its ring road that circles a large part of the city. On one ticket, one could go around as many times as one wanted, but of course, most people had destinations they had to alight at. However, I was one of those fortunate ones who did not have to get off anywhere.

On holidays especially, this used to be one of my favourite pastimes. To take a text and sit on the last window-seat of this bus and read as the city went past my window. Watching the different people get on and off in different combinations. This is by far the largest ensemble I have witnessed in my life.

If I live in any city long enough, this is something I definitely engage in. To take a public transport for a jaunt around that city, taking with me a play that speaks at least broadly about the world of that city.

For a theatre-maker, the greatest paradox of exploring the space of a city for its culture is that the people whom theatre champions often do not or cannot come to the theatre.

Urban spaces have evolved as sites of ghettoization, where the funders of theatre live far away from those whose stories need to be told most urgently. And the theatres are invariably built closer to where the funders are, usually the city's centre where the lesser-privileged ones do not live. In a way, our theatre buildings echo the problems of the liberal project. That its intentions and manifestations are not in sync. That in a way we want revolution without the revolution. We want equality without giving up privilege.

World over, many theatre buildings take great pride in their liberal values. They are the theatres that programme multicultural work, whose walls don posters of classic plays with leads played by actors of colour or other minority identities – and yet their audiences are predominantly made of those with the identity of privilege. This, I believe, is a deep-rooted problem because theatre aesthetics have evolved keeping the same identity in mind. In a way, the missing chapter of Aristotle's *Poetics* is 'Capital'. Whoever holds capital has had the opportunity to define taste, to define whose stories need to be told and also has had the opportunity to carry out the moral cleansing of the liberal project.

I believe the rise of right-wing politics in recent times is linked to this demographical paradox of audiences in major theatres of the world. We are largely preaching to the converted. By and large, we are all up for the same critique that Gunter Grass subjects Brecht to in his play, *The Plebeians Rehearse the Uprising*. That as the revolution was happening outside, the theatre building was rehearsing the past revolutions.

Nietzsche is known to have said that the gap between Voltaire and Rousseau is the unfinished business of the Enlightenment. He was referring to how Voltaire, despite being a great philosopher, kept himself in modest means, whereas Rousseau went on to capitalize in business and dealt in expensive trade in the Swiss Court, especially of watches. Unlike Voltaire, the theoretical framework in which Rousseau operated had no bearing on his personal choices.

I believe the same unfinished business applies in theatre.

III

After a few days of commuting with *The Coloured Museum*, one morning, I told the church lady that I was willing to go to her church with her.

There were two reasons for this. First, I have always loved church music and I had gotten to know that Black church music was quite different. That gospel and the blues had emanated from there. Second, a significant part of Naipaul's brilliant book *A Turn in the South* is about him looking at Black churches in the south of the United States. After these many years, unfortunately I cannot remember the name of that lady, but that weekend she did take me to her church and the music was indeed extraordinary.

Ritual performances always hold a very specific kind of energy, which many theatre-makers deeply desire to capture in a play. However, the greatest ingredient of ritual is not faith but physical memory. From a very young age, people go to congregations of all kinds with their parents, siblings and the community at large. When they participate in a ritual, the energy comes from a collective unbroken thread of practice. One's body knows the moves; one's voice knows the songs. It is extremely hard to create this rationally in a rehearsal space unless one casts people who are used to the rituals of the community they are representing.

Grotowski training in a way aspires to do exactly this. To use ritual as a performative tool. It delinks religion from achieving this level of ritual energy.

I have had the opportunity to see performances in Buddhist Tibetan theatre tradition in monasteries, Karbala rituals of Muslims, *Ramlila* and Black church music. All exceptional and very powerful. And I do not think I have ever seen a neutral secular liberal theatre-school that can teach a performer how to perform like that. As an atheist, I have no qualms that religion has given us good performance practices, particularly in music, although extremely questionable theories of origin and moral codes.

Coming out of the church that afternoon, I thanked that lady for the opportunity to see her church. She gave me a Bible and blessed me. Later that evening, I met some young Black artists on another friend's terrace in Brooklyn. Over food and drinks, we discussed Black theatre in New York City and also what *The Coloured Museum* meant to them now.

The most exciting conversation was around Aimé Césaire's adaptation of Shakespeare's *The Tempest*. How Césaire in this version tells the story particularly from the perspective of Caliban and Ariel, both slaves to Prospero. And how the difference between their ideological positions reflects that between Martin Luther King and Malcolm X.

Both Caliban and Ariel want freedom from Prospero, but Ariel wants it through non-violent methods, willing to wait till Prospero develops a conscience. However, Caliban is convinced that Prospero as a master will never develop that conscience. Caliban rejects everything he has received from Prospero over the years. The names he has been given, what he has been made to believe he is, the duties and the roles that have been assigned to him. In fact, Caliban's greatest fear is that he would internalize these lies given by his master so much that he would begin to believe in them himself and begin to live them out.

This internalization of lies is inimical to the self-assertion and determination of any oppressed community. We see characters recognizing this and turning against it in some of the Hallmark plays that talk about race. Lorraine Hansberry's *A Raisin in the Sun* and *Les Blancs*, August Wilson's *The Piano Lesson*, Athol Fugard's *'Master Harold' . . . and the Boys*, Wole Soyinka's *The Road* – all present characters who revolt against racism by rejecting the sense of self they have been provided.

That evening with these young Black theatre-workers in Brooklyn, I was getting an invaluable lesson on the issue of race in America. These were young people who were introducing me to the deep racial anxieties within American theatre. I was discussing with them issues of caste in India and how in India too most plays are essentially stories about upper-caste protagonists.

Whenever we talk of caste and race together, there are two views. One, that caste and race are two different things altogether. And the second, that they are co-revolutions in the making.

In a landmark judgement in the United States in 1896, *Plessy vs. Ferguson*, which upheld the constitutionality of racial segregation laws for public facilities, the lone dissenting judge wrote that the ruling was unconstitutional since 'there is no caste' in America. Hence, there was no systematic discrimination built into its society as it is in Hinduism.

This, of course, is not true.

Everywhere I have been, theatre is a place that challenges systematic institutionalized oppression. However, we are all aware that being a large system, it itself is often a carrier of these multiple institutionalized oppressions.

Lolita Chakrabarti's brilliant play *Red Velvet* tells the heartbreaking true story of an African American actor, Ira Aldridge, who arrived in London to play Othello. One of the most gifted actors on the American stage, he still left America to escape the racist nature of its theatre world and arrived in England to replace a white actor who was playing Othello at Covent Garden and was unable to continue. His arrival led to such furore that the theatre was nearly burnt. Audiences were all willing to empathize with the Moor on stage, his racial anxieties and challenges, but in reality, if a Black man played Othello, this was their reaction. This was in 1833.

Today the issue is far more complicated in my view. First, no theatre would directly accept any discrimination. And almost no theatregoer would accept that their theatregoing would be adversely affected if the profile of the actors or the plays changes to include people of minority identities. However, anyone who has ever programmed for theatre knows that there are categories that contain such representation. Categories called 'Diversity', 'Inclusion', 'International' and so on. The 'Normal' of theatre is not among these categories. The programme of any big theatre in Europe can show us where the money is spent.

In my view, the issue does not always stem from lack of intention but often from the dreadful cycle of 'theatre becoming a mirror to society'. If this is the case, it is extremely vital that theatre becomes not only a mirror but an X-ray machine. That it does not show us our cosmetics but our bones. That it shows us our ulcers, our rot and our assumptions.

The bourgeois tragedy is perhaps the most played theatre on this planet, closely followed by the bourgeois comedy in which only personal life-situations are at stake. This is often passed off as 'simple' comedy. Well-meaning laughter in which one leaves one's 'brains' outside. A kind of comedy or tragedy that one can purely feel and not have to think about, because there is already enough dread in the world. I believe the fact that we have to take trains and buses to make sense of *The Coloured Museum* and *A Raisin in the Sun* is because there simply isn't enough dread in the programming.

James Baldwin made a brilliant point about identity politics once in a television debate. Paul Weiss, a white philosophy professor from Yale, told him that they had more in common with each other than two Black men or two white men who do not have love for literature or philosophy. That being Black or white was not the only measure of one's identity and that Baldwin was reducing everything to a singular identity problem.

Baldwin replied to this by saying that whether a white man has a Black friend or a liberal white teacher has a good Black pupil is immaterial to one's experience of America. That a Black man's experience of America was not the experience of having a white friend. It was about having white institutions turned against the Black man. That one's experience of America as a Black man was of being told by Robert Kennedy that in forty years, Black people could imagine having a Black president, and hence, America was doing better. The irony of it: a Johnny-come-lately like Robert Kennedy, who was already on his way to the presidency, telling Black people, who had been around for four hundred years, that they would have to wait another forty years before white people would 'allow' them to become the president.

The big question Baldwin is asking here is essentially a Marxist one. How will the means of sustenance change for Black people if they are still fixing the race problem case by case? It is here that identity politics and Marxist thought converge. Both must recognize that identity is vital to what one has access to in this world, and yet, both must strive to ultimately change the conditions for the many.

In modern life, there are no Uncle Vanyas and no Lopakhins. Such individual tragedy is no longer reflective of the society. Modern dramaturgy always needs to account for a 'People' because we are now a world full of choruses. There are no protagonists who are fulfilling a single destiny. Hence, theatre also needs to move away from 'diversity' to plurality, and this is not an easy thing to do.

When we were staging *Pah-la*, a play set in contemporary Tibet, at Royal Court Theatre, there was a great furore over social media that not a single Tibetan actor had been cast. The fact was that during the auditions no Tibetan actor had been found who was acting on the professional stage in the UK. The few that auditioned did not make the cut, and hence, were not selected. Anyway, the Tibetan production of the play in India was going to be with an all-Tibetan cast.

A campaign was started against Royal Court, spearheaded particularly by some of the Tibetan members who had auditioned and failed, posting pictures of those who had been cast, calling them Chinese actors. Now this is where in reality the question of identity becomes more complex and needs greater nuance. The actors who were in the production took deep offence at being singularly labelled Chinese when they were actually from several parts of East Asia and were primarily second-generation British citizens.

The theatre was surprised at the reaction when it had worn its best diversity hat and cast actors of 'East-Asian' origin as opposed to casting white British actors in Tibetan and Chinese roles as a lesser theatre would have done. The Tibetans had several arguments between themselves about whether this was a racial oversight or there were genuinely no Tibetan stage actors in UK, and how acting in cinema and film was completely different with very different levels of commitment required over large periods of time.

From their own point of view, all three parties had improved upon the existing blind spots of casting in the UK. However, it was not good enough for the other group's perception of what is the ethnic group in question. Is it Tibetans? Is it East-Asians? Or just everyone who is not Chinese?

I have been to New York City several times after my stint in Lincoln Centre. I have made friends with some incredible Black American playwrights. I have had some extraordinary Black American students who have written extremely sharp and nuanced work in class.

Now when I go to New York City, my frame of reference is no longer *Home Alone*. *The Coloured Museum* as a reference turned out to be far more accurate.

And in a way, this realigning of axis is the job of all art, particularly the theatre. To not become a mirror of the theatre-house but of the society that should be sitting inside it.

Theatre has always been a place where the voiceless have found voice. It is extremely important that in times to come these voices are heard more, these faces become more visible, but also that this is led by structural change and not just mere representation.

Ultimately, I think, reading groups in theatre that decide which plays will be put up and which won't shouldn't always meet indoors.

When in doubt about whether a play should be programmed or not, the plays need to be taken out.

They need to be read while travelling.

If theatre remains fixed, it will become exactly what it tries to overthrow.

A dogma that goes unquestioned.

It needs to keep giving us new lenses and new plays to make sense of our world.

It needs to be programmed by Caliban. Prospero must be present for the dialogue.

9

Hamidur Rehman

A journey through Bangladesh and Germany. A journey about a journey

I

Bengalis have two names. A *daak naam*, the name used to call us at home, and a *bhalo naam*, the good name used outside our homes by the rest of the world. In many ways, this story is about the clash of these two names and the different meanings each name can hold in one's life.

Sometime before 2011, Hamidur Rehman – or Shobuj (meaning 'green' in Bangla), as was his *daak naam*, stood before Hamburg's Deutsches Schauspielhaus and clicked a picture. It was a picture for a news article on him and his journey. A journey that had brought him from Bangladesh's Gazipur district to Hamburg via Malaysia and Italy. He had tried to seek asylum as a political refugee but had been denied several times. And so, he decided to cross Greenland on foot in order to reach Canada. Midway, he collapsed on the snow and if it had not been for a helicopter that spotted him, he would have died that day on the snow thousands and thousands of miles away from home, where it doesn't snow even in fables.

That Hamidur survived that crossing was a sheer stroke of luck. It is for these incidents, a member of his family told me, that one wants to believe in something beyond ourselves. A few months later, a night before his last asylum hearing, he called up a Christian priest. But before that priest could reach him, Hamidur committed suicide. In a small town in Germany. In a colourless room. And it is for these reasons one finds it also hard to be a believer, added that same family member.

Hamidur's story came to me through two German friends and colleagues. Sophia Stepf and Konradin Kunze. Along with Lisa Stepf, they are the founders of Flinn Works in Berlin. They told me about his story, sent the news article and then asked me if I was keen on researching the story with them in Bangladesh and devising it together.

I readily agreed.

The project was exciting, and I had always wanted to visit Bangladesh from where my paternal family had come to this side of what was still Undivided India then in 1946. A journey that changed the story of my family forever. My father escaped with his family to the western part of the state of Bengal, foreseeing major riots due to the partition of India at independence, leaving his ancestral home in Noakhali that became part of East Pakistan in 1947. The place where he grew up, Dhaka, became the capital of that new country. By the time he died in 1984, East Pakistan had become Bangladesh after a 'Liberation War' against Pakistan by Bengalis of East Pakistan in 1971 with the support of the Indian army. And so, while my father died in independent India, the country he was born in had changed names and maps thrice. While I was keen on exploring Hamidur's story, I also wanted to go to Dhaka to revisit my own family's past where, I am told, my grandfather had been a professor at Dhaka Medical College in the 1900s.

Like most refugee families, the stories are highly debatable. No one is now alive to testify the truth about anything that we know about the lives of my family in Dhaka or Noakhali. My grandfather, Dr Kaminikanto Majumdar, was one of the members of the team that found the vaccine for 'Kala azar', or black cholera, according to my uncle. Refugee families are full of stories of past glory. I wanted to go back and see what I could for myself.

I was being given an opportunity to understand that journey which has shaped my entire life by working in the theatre on another man's journey in the 2000s. Both from in and around Dhaka city.

In a way, all of theatre is about journeys. Every epic involves someone travelling. Moses parts the ocean and climbs a mountain. Mohammad travels from Mecca to Medina and thus sets off the Islamic calendar. Buddha leaves home and wanders in the forest, Rama goes into exile for fourteen years and Odysseus fulfils his destiny by leaving home and then returning after twenty years.

When I heard about Hamidur, I knew instantly that he had also been part of an epic journey. His story was no less significant than that of any of these epic heroes. And yet, no one would know of him. He would be lost in a small article in a paper.

We would be bringing his story to theatre. Bringing him back to life for some time. Play this piece in Bangladesh and Germany, Dhaka and Hamburg. To tell a story which connects these two places through the story of this man. Hamidur.

Like in the beginning of any theatre project, I was full of questions. My most pressing question is still unanswered in many ways. Why did Hamidur so desperately want to be in Europe? What was he trying to escape so badly? Why could he not come back to Bangladesh, if not specifically to his village in Gazipur? The journeys from war-torn parts of the world like Syria and Iraq are understandable. They are about choosing between life and death. But why did Hamidur feel he needed to make this journey in a period of relative peace and prosperity in Bangladesh? His surrounding areas were surely witnessing political turmoil and he was being targeted in it, but what was the reason for him to want so desperately to leave Bangladesh itself? The fact that these questions could be asked and explored during the making of this play interested me enormously.

Tony Kushner's *Angels in America* opens with a rabbi's monologue at the funeral of an old Jewish woman. He speaks of her as someone who had carried her world on her back from Russia to America. Of how such epic journeys were no longer possible. That, in a sense, she was the last of the Mohicans.

Angels in America is one of my all-time favourite plays. But over time, I have found myself questioning this sentence over and over again. Kushner's rabbi is right, of course, but perhaps only for the West and that too up until the time of the recent war in Ukraine. Perhaps such journeys have not been seen in the Western world since the late 1950s till now. However, this is exactly the story of all those migrants who brave oceans, hostile armed forces, mountains and barbed wires to go from one country to another. To escape the tyranny of dictators planted by Western superpowers, the tyranny of World Bank loans, the tyranny of aspiration metered out through adverts, Hollywood and HBO. These people go West and do everything to adapt and fit in. And then they love remembering the past. One of the great epidemics of the twentieth and twenty-first century, in my view, is the 'fatigue of the West'. The continuous inescapable presence it has and its demand that everyone fits in.

In a way, the only way to escape this fatigue is to embrace it. To want to half-belong. To stay in a small ethnic community in a large Western city. To never meet anyone except each other. To celebrate festivals in little gardens and qualify in society as 'diversity'. To never be able to belong completely and to never be able to come back completely. To wake up one day and realize that there are only two stories you have left to tell. That of someone who misses home and that of someone who is not at home here.

If the Western world continues to tell all the stories in the years to come, it wouldn't be surprising to see many plays set in living rooms. But if the rest of the world could tell its own tales, stages would be filled with tops of trains, luggage compartments of airplanes and boxes in boats and dinkies. We would have to find the means to effectively stage 'walks' and not conversations in living rooms.

To not travel by choice but to have to travel. Not for business or leisure but as oxygen. To survive.

We have to remember that the best thing that can happen to many people in the world is to become 'Diaspora'. Diaspora is the name for those who survived. It is not a noun. It's a verb. It means to be alive elsewhere.

Hamidur had done everything in his power to become this diaspora. Ultimately, when he couldn't, he killed himself. This bothered me then, and it bothers me even today. Every time I board an airplane. Every time my phone picks up the Wi-Fi at Heathrow Airport or JFK on landing.

II

The three of us went to Dhaka and then to Hamidur's village in Gazipur district, an hour from Dhaka city, to interview the various people in his life. The first and most important connection was with his sister, Sadia Swatee. Sophia had made this connection before we reached. Even now, after nearly eight years, Sadia calls me sometimes and sends me gifts and books of her own writing, like she would to a brother. Without her, we could not have proceeded.

Sadia wanted us to tell this story in the theatre as much as we wanted to. But I think all of us had different points of entry. Sophia and Konradin were appalled by what Germany had done to Hamidur, I was looking for an answer to my question and Sadia wanted to keep her brother alive in this way. Her family had seen him return home only in a body bag. She informed us that he was working for Awami League and was essentially trying to counter the atrocities and illiberal impositions of BNP (Bangladesh Nationalist Party) workers in Gazipur.

Once again, like in many other places, we had a few things in common. We shared the same mother tongue, and we ate together and drank tea together. Once again, I found that which has never failed: that people trust theatre. They may not trust the government, or non-government agencies, or even big-budget cinema and television. But when they meet a small theatre group, they believe these people have no vested interest other than telling the story.

Sadia took us to her village in Gazipur, some miles away from Dhaka city. We went to Hamidur's grave there and then to their house. It turned out to be a small hut where we met – among other people – their mother. Ammi.

She spoke neither English nor German and so conversed with the team through translations. But like with Sadia, I could speak to Ammi directly in Bangla, even though there were distinct differences between our dialects. Speaking to her, I soon realized that I was sitting in front of possibly the most important audience I would ever have in my life.

She had tears in her eyes when she spoke of Hamidur. And she kept looking at the three of us together. And this is when I realized two important things about this project, and theatre in general, which were corroborated later. The first realization came with the question she asked me as she very keenly observed Konradin,

Sophia and me together. She asked me in Bangla something to the effect of 'How are they?' I understood she was not asking me how Sophia and Konradin were as people. She knew that they were the ones behind this project, who were putting in their everything to be able to pose before their own people the question of why her son had to kill himself. What she really wanted to know was how were they with me. She had known Hamidur was in Germany and must have imagined the kind of people he would be surrounded with there. She was asking me this question in that context. And I told her they were good, that it was not a problem.

Many months later, when Konradin and I performed in Dhaka, she came to us after the performance and held the two of us for some time. And I felt that something had resolved for her after seeing that it is possible for us to work together. To talk to each other. To understand each other. Theatre had given her a model of the world that was very far away from what they would show her on cinema or television. Finally, she had a way of knowing that it was possible for us to meet. That what her Shobuj had hoped for was real and possible. And I realized then that theatre was a way of understanding the possibilities of this world as much for this elderly woman living in a hut in Gazipur in Bangladesh as it is for a regular theatregoer in London or Berlin.

The second realization came with how she was looking at me specifically. She had understood from the beginning that in the performance, for most parts, I would be playing her Bangla-speaking son. This was the hardest audition of my life. She was not merely looking for similarities in our appearances (although coincidentally, I do resemble Hamidur quite a lot). What she was really looking for were signs of her son in me.

I have never in my life felt that close to an audience member before whom I was going to perform to. She treated me with enormous love. For when I performed, she would be seeing in me her son one more time. While for Kondradin, Sophia and me, this project was about attempting to understand something about the time we live in, for her it was an opportunity to relive some moments with her son through our play. I realized from her quest to find Hamidur in me the other fundamental thing about theatre, which is about time.

Theatre has three concurrent and paradoxical relationships with time. First, it is about a model of the world, its possibilities, and hence, about a possible future. At the heart of every good play, whether set in the future or not, lies an argument for the future. Edward Bond had put this wonderfully: 'Plays young people write, act in and watch are the blueprints of the world they will have to live in.'

Second, along with the future, at the heart of every piece of theatre is also its exact opposite: the past. People world over go to theatre to remember. To understand the world by revisiting what has happened and looking at it with some distance now. Like Hamidur's mother, they come to theatre nurturing a dream of seeing the dead resurrected once again.

In fact, across the world, several theatre traditions are about recalling the ancestors. Actors in these traditions, like Theyyam in Kerala (a southern state in India), are in fact not known for their acting skills but their ability to get possessed. Gods, ancestors, memories come alive in plays because human beings are blessed and cursed at the same time with memory. No other species is known to be able to recall history to the number of generations that we can. To associate a piece of land to a name many generations ago. This fundamental need to remember manifests itself in theatre everywhere.

The third and vital mechanics of time in the theatre is that ultimately it is about the present. Every theatre-performer knows that the only way to inhabit the past and the future is by being completely in the present. Only when we are completely in the present is it possible for us to live forever. Every moment holds the key to understanding the future and the past.

The presence of these three kinds of time together is what gives theatre its unique temporal quality that is reminiscent of life. For in life too we exist in all three times concurrently.

We interviewed several people in Bangladesh. Many of them spoke of how brave Hamidur was. How he had once fought against a dogmatic school teacher in order to protect some girls from their neighbourhood. How he had risked his life several times for others. However, we could only interview one person who had something to say against him. And that person was close to BNP.

This is something which worried me a lot till the end of the play. The fact that we were not meeting more people who were BNP supporters and who might have had a problem with Hamidur. In my other research that I have done in other parts of the world, I have always believed it is very important to speak also with people who have an alternate view to where the sympathies of the story might lie. It enriches everything, the argument for and against. In fact, in this case, it would have made a compelling case for what Hamidur was trying to escape.

However, we were in a very peculiar situation. People knew we were about to make a play on Hamidur Rehman. He was to be the protagonist. Sadia Swatee, an urban person, and that too from the media, was with us. Besides, we were also two white people out of three. Konradin and Sophia were not imposing or intruding at all, but understandably interviews in South Asia completely change in the presence of interviewers, especially if they are white.

There was no way of escaping this situation at that time. We had very few days in Gazipur and Dhaka, and I found the research wanting. It gave us a depth of field to our story but I felt it didn't allow us to justify why Hamidur had left. I also knew that sympathy for Hamidur would come easily in the liberal theatre-watching circles in Germany. And personally, very few things bother me more than the simplistic sympathy of Western audiences for characters who come from the Third World. It always absolves everyone of any responsibility. One feels guilty about not having protected a good-hearted, simple, unargumentative, innocent lesser-privileged character and then one goes home. One of the traps of capitalism and imperial history is to equate the poor with simplicity and the rich with complexity. One needs to have the most compelling arguments and not just deal in feelings, especially in plays about non-Western themes.

I wanted our Hamidur to have to argue. To come across as someone who had to fight in both Gazipur and the Western world to be understood.

Right from Shakespeare's time, theatre has suffered from the disease of making the poor fools and the rich the people with arguments and language. With the exception of the character of Fool in *King Lear*, one would have to struggle really hard to find a single good argument coming from a poorer person or a person from the Orient, which was not mystical in some way. The East has been doomed in Western culture to deal with its Orientalism. That there are simple and yet wise people roaming the Orient, who do not have a tradition of argument or rationality but do have some deeper wisdom, is one of the easiest ways to diminish the intellectual and argumentative history of a people. The worst way

to belittle someone is to praise their convenient image as opposed to examining their reality.
I absolutely did not want this to happen to Hamidur. Neither did Konradin nor Sophia, I am sure. However, I am not sure if consciously we were thinking about this together in the same way. And this is one of the most important aspects of any cross-cultural collaboration. That we can all be well-meaning but the real challenge is to be able to see not just each other's point of view but also each other's vantage point. To see why are we interested in different things in the same collaborative project.

III

When we got back to India, our rehearsals in Bangalore went wonderfully initially. Konradin had created an incredible cardboard model-set of the different locations that Hamidur had visited, and this was projected using a video camera. He has incredible ease with building things with his hands and is a brilliant theatre mind. And Sophia is a wonderful dramaturg, with an incredible amount of experience in translating cross-cultural references on stage. So long as we were telling what we had heard and read, it was going very well.

The problem began for me when we started devising new material that referred to the material we already had at hand. I kept feeling an unease that our improvisations had no voice that could be critical of Hamidur. None which asked whether he really went away because of political pressure or because he just wanted a good life in Europe. This was a vital question from my (or any South Asian's) point of view as far as this story was concerned. It changed how we perceived his death. Was it desperation to survive or to do well in life?

I think the fundamental weight of this question comes from the fraught relation one has as an Asian with the 'sense of being' one sees in Western dramatic traditions. Since Plato, the central thesis of the West has been that there is a concrete *I* or self at the centre of the human experience. The path of human life in this world view is to find that I. Hence from *Iliad* to *Odyssey*, from the Theban plays to *King Lear*, there is a quest to find who that I is and what is moral within that definite sense of I.

However, in Zen, Taoism, Buddhism, Vedanta and several other Asian traditions, the thing at the centre in not *being* but *nothingness*. The quest of Rama in *Ramayana* or of Milarepa in *The Tale of Milarepa* is not to find that essential self but to transcend it. To go, in fact, towards nothingness.

This has shaped the fundamental discourse around material well-being differently in Asia. This is not to Orientalize it again and assert that material philosophy has no place in the scheme of things there. Ambedkar, Periyar, Marx, Nishida, Ramanuja, Nagarjuna, Gandhi, Adi Shankaracharya, Lao-Tze and Mao are no less influential on Indian, Chinese and Japanese thought than any non-materialist doctrine. In fact, even a non-materialist doctrine like Gandhism endorses rituals of material assertion, like making one's own salt and weaving one's own cloth, as means of liberation.

However, while a purely material quest would be understood as a necessity in Bangladesh and India, at the same time, it would be viewed with considerable scepticism within such a society. For unlike the West, these are cultures that consider fulfilment in material terms to be separate from the higher spiritual goal of transcending one's being. And hence, I felt that Hamidur would be scrutinized unfairly by the Eastern audiences if we viewed him only as a subject looking for a liberation of 'being' in the Western sense of that term, where material fulfilment is not seen separate from fulfilling one's destiny. Hamidur was a radical in his own society, but that might not mean that he had also rejected his culture's quest for something essentially non-material.

Our rehearsal in this light grew more and more difficult as days went by, and we did not exactly know what the problem was. Then one day, we were having trouble again with a scene, and we stopped work to discuss it. In the ensuing debate about whether we were questioning Hamidur's need to stay in Germany or not, I realized that my colleagues were using the term 'political worker' again and again to justify his escape from Bangladesh. And it was exactly this phrase that was making me think over and over again that we did not have the entire story. I asked them what they thought a political worker does. To which Konradin replied that a political worker was someone who went to houses and gave out leaflets and thus built political discourse in the community.

It is here that the penny dropped. In South Asia, this is absolutely not the idea of a political worker. In South Asia, a political worker for most parts is someone who is potentially violent (justified or not), who potentially has a fraught relationship with many and can even be antisocial. We suddenly realized that what stood between us and realizing the play we could make together was the meaning of this one phrase. We recognized clearly now that while our politics was very similar, our political cultures were very different.

Collaborative work is like this. It is not the big things that stop it, for it is very easy to agree on morals, aesthetics and even vanity of stage time and such things. What is hard is wanting to say the same thing but understanding the words inside it completely differently. I told them what I thought a political worker was, and then we had to sit down and feel that incredible moment in a cross-cultural rehearsal. A moment in which you realize that you have found something that you can never resolve. Because no matter what you do, you cannot change where you come from, what you have seen, heard, smelt and tasted. And this is the key difference between creating theatre alone as a writer-director and creating material through a collaborative process.

I was no more an authority on Hamidur than they were. Even though I spoke his language, I knew nothing extra about him. However, their sympathy for him was automatic because of their vantage point. However, I wanted to feel no sympathy. I wanted Hamidur to argue. And win. I wanted him to challenge the audience in Hamburg and Dhaka equally. I wanted to win the argument for my father and grandfather and for people like Hamidur who are invisible in Western cities till one reaches a grocery story. I wanted Hamburg to meet a complex Hamidur. My friends wanted that too, but I suppose they did not share my anxieties about him being perceived as a victim. I did not want him to be a victim at all. There is only one thing that annoys me more than racist disdain – and that is racist sympathy.

But I knew I was sitting in a room with two people who are not racist by any stretch of imagination. The question before us now was how could we pull this together. Our research had been conducted with due diligence but keeping in mind only their idea of a political worker, as someone who gave out leaflets. This was not my idea at all of how Hamidur would have been seen as a political worker in his village, and I felt we needed to interview more members of BNP who were opposed to Hamidur. But we had an opening date now, and how would we be able to bridge that research gap before that?

We must have had two or three very difficult sessions of rehearsal following this, but in my view, it was also very liberating to know what the issue was. It was next to impossible to call the show off and go back to Gazipur to do more research. At the same time, I was indeed finding it impossible to put my name down as a creator of this piece since I was increasingly uncomfortable about the one-sidedness of the content.

When I look back at this moment, what is really interesting about it is how the nature of our disagreement belies any scepticism one might have about a process like this without being a part of it. Here we were, a South Asian with roots in Bangladesh insisting that we had to know more about Hamidur's political activity and that he should not be a victim alone in our play, whereas the two Germans in the room were keen on protecting Hamidur dramaturgically. This is the beauty of theatre. People often ask me about collaborative processes and I often tell them that I have never been in a rehearsal where theatre people have wanted to belittle each other. I like to believe that theatre is here to question the powerful and protect the oppressed. Konradin, Sophia and I were, in our own ways, doing absolutely the right thing. We were fighting for Hamidur on opposite sides but on the right sides of our personal histories.

Eventually, we agreed that I will be credited as an actor and not as a devising collaborator. However, if we got more research done and incorporated it into the project, I could take credit as a collaborator. I can imagine this must have been hard on them because they had really wanted me to come as an equal creator. But the contours of the project were such that it would be impossible to pull off what I wanted in terms of time and money. And this is something quite hard to get by in internationally funded projects of this scale. They assume a getting-in, research, rehearsal and getting-out process. They are approved often by institutions who support art but from outside. Several times in international scenarios, I have felt that the funders are well-meaning but they don't differentiate between a theatre project and a software project in terms of their reporting and execution.

Once we got this arrangement between us sorted out, the rehearsals went quite smoothly. Also, bear in mind that at this time we were all living together in my house. There was no love lost. We understood that we might disagree on what needs to happen to the narrative hereon, but we were in agreement as people and had the same respect for each other as collaborators. And in a way, I felt extremely liberated to be able to place my entire attention on Hamidur as an actor. Perhaps I needed to play him more closely to answer the questions I was seeking to address. Whereas Konradin and Sophia needed to do what they were doing.

IV

A few months later, we went back to Dhaka to perform the show. To what could turn out to be the most extraordinary performance I have been a part of.

Before the show at the Goethe Institute in Dhaka, several technicians and carpenters told me in Bangla that I should really take this opportunity and learn from the white man. There was a German folding-table at the institute and while one of the technicians there was setting it up for the projector, he said to me: 'Can you see this table? It folds so well. They have made this table. It will take us hundreds of years to make a table like this.'

I smiled and agreed.

Then he said to me: 'This is Saheb's brain. They are really better than us. Try your best today.'

I always find these situations wonderfully amusing. At the deeply embedded sense we South Asians have about the superiority of the West. As the day passed and I spoke to the technicians, I was thinking what this play would mean to them when they see Konradin and me together. When they see me playing Hamidur and even pushing Konradin in a scene. What would it mean when the expectations are turned on stage. Would it resolve the racial tension or further compel everyone to think about class? I could push my co-actor but would that change their relationship to the experience of racial submission. Both Hamidur and I came from here. We were neither in London nor Berlin. We were not migrants. We were here in our home. That home might be Bangladesh, India or Pakistan, but the audience will still register it as a *sahib* on stage standing with a brown man. The entire day was thus like being in an Athol Fugard play like *Playland* or *'Master Harold' . . . and the Boys*, which combines race with stories of the working class.

In the evening, just before the opening, I saw Sadia and Ammi walk in and take the first row, the mother looking for her son. After some time, Konradin and I took the stage. We had taken stage in a similar manner in the other shows at Hamburg and Bremerhaven in Germany, Bangalore in India and Chittagong in Bangladesh. But this was completely different.

I have always felt that the way audiences sit on their chairs, or on the floor, says something fundamental about their relationship to the play they are watching. Not whether the play is good or bad but what it means in that culture. Often the expression 'on the edge of the seat' refers to a state of exhilaration about some kind of mystery or moment of comic tension about to unfurl. The edge of the seat is deemed to be a location of possibility. That from here anything could happen on stage that would be very exciting. But I find this expression extremely misleading.

In moments of great tension or possibility, people could also be too tensed to move. They could sink in or retract in horror. Gender might play a huge role in many cultures, in deciding who automatically occupies the edge of the seat and who does not. The variables are far too many.

Also, there could be deeper ways of feeling and watching a play than by perpetually judging its worth by its ability to exhilarate. Exhilaration might be somewhat desirable sometimes, but overall a play that continuously exhilarates is certainly not be the best model for all the possibilities of a live performance.

In my view, audiences watch plays with either their legs or their shoulders. They either plant their feet deep and move around that axis, or they settle into the area just below the shoulder and pivot around it. When the audience is learning something about the state of the world or a potential future from a play, it tends to remain light on its feet. When a play resurrects the dead, its feet are planted. A performance is seen and processed by the entire body.

Thus, while watching a play, our body is participating in a continuous dance most of the time. We are continuously making small adjustments to our posture based on where the play is at a particular moment of time. In my view, if we were to map through a device the movements of an attentive audience, seated on chairs or on the floor, we would be able to have a sense of how much of the play is about an idea of the future and how much it is about resurrecting their own past.

The play did very well while it ran. Our shows were extremely appreciated in all the places we performed. We could not do a very long run due to logistical issues of being in two different countries, subsequent funding and so on. However, for me, the highlight undoubtedly was Hamidur's mother holding Konradin and me and calling me Shobuj. To be honest, that was enough for me. Something had been answered as far as I was concerned.

Sadia and Ammi have stayed in touch with me since. They have sent gifts, books and sweets to me and my family. They have called me *Bhaiya* (brother) and Shobuj. We have exchanged sarees and poems.

Some years later, Konradin and Sophia presented a paper on this play in Washington, though I could not be present there. I have always asked myself if I should have agreed to stay as a collaborator and worked with the material we had, instead of changing my participation to a non-writing actor. I find myself conflicted.

As a theatre-maker, I was indeed responsible for this play along with them and perhaps I should have owned up to what we had. However, I was not opposed to it if we had more material and were ready to work on it. Time and money would not have allowed us to do so immediately, but in time it would have been possible.

But the bigger issue for me was that I did not want to feel that I had created a narrative that presented Hamidur, a man much like myself, as a victim. I did not want the West's sympathy. For myself, for my father's family and for my grandparents, who had worked on a British team to discover the vaccine for black cholera and then died after a mindless partition of the subcontinent by a line drawn by a British man called Radcliffe who lived here for two weeks. Literally two weeks.

And for Hamidur.

I truly believe that someday we will have another shot at telling Hamidur's story. When we will also be able to establish the connection between BNP and American aid to Bangladesh. When we will be able to mourn not only Hamidur but also the international system that creates Hamidurs in the world.

Theatre gave us an incredible possibility to delve into this complex story and perform in three countries. I am sure it will give us another chance to complete it.

As I write this, last evening, after seven months, I connected with Sadia. She told me she had written something on Hamidur – and that Ammi died this July.

I slept with Ammi in my thoughts. Her calling me Shobuj after the show in Dhaka is the kind of moment for which world over human beings have gathered around fire and told each other stories. To remember the dead and to see them again and finally have a closure for the road ahead. To know that we make art to reconcile memory and desire. To recognize that though Hamidur died, for his mother, 'Shobuj' will always be alive.

The *bhalo naam* was consumed by bureaucracy. The *daak naam* was what he really was.

In the end, Shobuj freed Hamidur from the burden of his *bhalo naam*.

Part III

Other Geographies

10

Lessons in pausing

From a theatre in West Africa to a monastery in the Himalayas

I

Ouagadougou, the capital of Burkina Faso in West Africa, is a city with one of the most extraordinary theatre cultures in the world. This city puts to rest the myth that people pursue art only once their other needs are met.

It is not that Ouagadougou does not have its share of wealthy individuals and families. Like most modern cities of economically developing or underdeveloped countries (Delhi, Mumbai, Dhaka, Manila etc.), it too has its pockets of relative wealth. But much like them, Ouagadougou too is marked by rampant poverty. But as my friend Luca Fusi who lives and works there told me, 'Burkinabe (the people of Burkina Faso) are not ashamed of poverty.' This was news to me, growing up in the Indian megalopolis of Delhi where by and large poverty is directly connected to lack of dignity.

It is here in Ouagadougou that I learnt one of the most important lessons about dramatic time.

One morning, our hosts, Luca Fusi and Ildevert, took us to Gambidi School of Performing Arts, a wonderful institution with departments of theatre, dance and music, and an active repertory. The school also has a theatre space where plays are staged regularly by its repertory and other groups from Ouagadougou.

Like most other performance spaces that we saw in Ouagadougou, Gambidi's theatre space is only half-covered. The audience area is open air while the stage has a roof over it, presumably to be able to hang some lights.

We were taking a look at the space when Ildevert said, 'Every evening at about eight pm an Ethiopian airlines aircraft passes over Gambidi. The sound of that aircraft is quite loud and, as you can see, there are no special acoustics here.'

'So, what happens then?' I asked.

Ildevert smiled sheepishly as he often does. 'As the plane arrives, everyone pauses for a few seconds. The players, the audience, everyone. Because there is nothing to be done about this situation. But they don't drop the play. No one talks, no cell phones are checked and no watches are looked at. Everybody holds the play together. It is everyone's responsibility to make the play work.'

There was unfortunately no performance happening in this theatre while we were there, so I could not see this extraordinary moment of silence in person, but I loved this story. Ildevert is a great master and one of the wisest people I have ever known in the world, and I knew he had taught me something important.

About dramatic time.

That in the theatre we the players are fundamentally getting into an agreement with the audience about 'what happens when nothing happens'.

The real play is in the gaps.

We come to the theatre to create gaps in time, in which we can experience and reflect on life rather than perfunctorily participate in it. In a sense, a live performance is a form of mindfulness.

It itself is an *active pause* from our day-to-day lives. Not a distraction but a lens that allows us to amplify our understanding of the rest of our life.

A moment on stage is only as good as the gap between this moment and the next.

Preetam Koilpillai, a brilliant Indian director who is also an outstanding piano player, had once told me while I was improvising as an actor, 'Listen. Listen to a note. And before this note gets over, you will know what the next note should be. But listen to the note you are creating. Don't rush it.'

Every culture, every dramatic tradition, treats time in completely different ways. The idea of time in Aristotle's *Poetics* does not apply to Zeami's treatise in Japan or the *Natya Shastra* in India.

There is no universal principle of how time needs to be structured, although certain dominant discourses of Aristotelian drama have been often positioned as being the norm world over. The direction of ideas, as it commonly happens, is decided by the colonial past of the world. Consequently, the European middle-class discourse about dramatic time being a form of compression has become the flawed bedrock of how dramatists need to treat time in a scene, in an act and a play. Everything else is seen as an experiment in comparison to the standard Aristotelian dramaturgy.

This is not a tenable idea if we look at what different theatre cultures do with dramatic time around the world. And this is directly related to how different cultures treat time in their day-to-day lives, in their rituals, in their way of structuring their society, their concept of death and, very importantly, their model of afterlife.

Theatre is directly connected to beliefs about life and death. In many cultures around the world, a performance is nothing less than a rite of passage between worlds. And conception of time works differently for a culture that believes we are at the end of time versus one that believes that finite time is a myth in the first place.

Even urgency has different meanings in different cultures. That is why in a certain kind of theatre that swears by Aristotelian dramatic writing, 'elaboration' is called 'exposition' and looked down upon, whereas in another kind of theatre that centres experience, the highest purpose of a performance is the elaboration of a moment. In such theatrical traditions such as Noh, Kabuki, Kathakali and Koodiyattam, plot is merely there for us to be able to elaborate the ideas that reflect life.

This difference in the treatment of time is not a binary. It depends on the particular culture in question and, I think, has to do with both religion and the interaction between rural and urban life in a given place.

II

There are today, in my view, three distinct cultures in the world.

The first culture is the *urban-urban*, in which city-bred people living in cities are completely absorbed in an industrial reality. Time here is measured to the nanosecond. People know the status of every delivery, every train, every cab and the length of every phone call to the last second. In these cultures, *time* as an entity is believed to have been mastered.

The theatre of this culture begins at a given time based on the mechanical or digital clock. There is a time to come into the theatre, a call sheet, a time log, a duration for each play that is predetermined to the level that the faders in the light booths are inscribed with time stamps that tells the technician how fast or slow a fade needs to be to the last millisecond.

This is a culture that uses the language of clocks and measurement even in the objects of its theatre because it runs on the bedrock of the assumption that the most fundamental unit of experience is measurable time.

The second culture is *rural-rural*. In this culture, theatre happens in the villages in largely traditional, non-industrial societies and the players are also from the countryside. This could also be the culture of smaller towns in places where industrialization is not the axiom of life. In such places, life and theatre reflect the availability of time. This availability is misconstrued by urban-urban cultures as being idle. However, if one lives in a rural-rural setting, one will realize there is in fact the hardship of a much more physically demanding existence and, at the same time, the opportunity to experience the present moment and space intensely. One is not looking for continuous distractions. One is not living one's life from one experience to another, expecting exhilaration at every moment.

The theatre in these cultures is often that of elaboration. Here the plot is known to people, the songs memorized and the movements internalized by the audience. Very often, this theatre is not competing with television or commercial cinema in the way that theatre of urban-urban cultures does. Here, people gather on certain days of the year, in specific seasons, often following a religious calendar to watch a performance. And the performances can last all night. Often, they last for months. People gather to watch these plays because watching these plays is part of the ritual

of existence. The dramaturgy of these plays does not rely on twists of the story or on clever dialogue.
Arundhati Roy writes beautifully in *The God of Small Things*:

> Kathakali discovered long ago that the secret of the Great Stories is that they have no secrets. The Great Stories are the ones you have heard and want to hear again. The ones you can enter anywhere and inhabit comfortably. They don't deceive you with thrills and trick endings. They don't surprise you with the unforeseen. They are as familiar as the house you live in. Or the smell of your lover's skin. You know how they end, yet you listen as though you don't. In the way that although you know that one day you will die, you live as though you won't. In the Great Stories you know who lives, who dies, who finds love, who doesn't. And yet you want to know again. That is their mystery and their magic.

It is also true that to be able to experience a story without twists and turns, one must also have space for elaboration in one's life. We can contend with content that is far from our experience. But form is deeply entrenched in existence. We can only experience a form on stage if that form is present in our lives.

However, 'time' is so fundamental to human experience that I think to accept a different sense of it, to be able to pause differently, is the final frontier of empathy. We can understand those who speak a different language, but we cannot understand those who remain silent differently.

The third and most significant modern movement in the world is the emergence of *urban-rural* theatre. The beginning of colonization in the last two centuries witnessed the phenomenon of performers of one culture travelling to other cultures, bringing with them their native performance traditions. The politics of the direction of this movement has been extremely bloody and obviously from the colonizer to the colonized.

The British rule brought to the world bourgeois middle-class theatre, which meant that the plight of the plantation owner had to be performed by the plantation worker. The man who slaved throughout the day in the plantations of the colonizer had to dress up in the colonizer's clothes and become a fool in the colonizer's plays in the evenings. He had to serve drinks to the master at night, as the master watched tragedies in which people like himself – well fed, well slept, rich, wealthy and with a benevolent god – had personal sorrows.

These plays were very often in sharp contrast to the plantation workers' plays in which one walked on coal, in which the gods got angry and in which co-villagers got possessed and frothed from the mouth. The violence of the master was veiled by the evening gowns of fictional people, whereas the suffering of the workers was veiled by the gradual criminalization of their performance traditions by the colonizers world over.

By the time the twentieth century arrived, 'theatre' was what the master did and 'superstition' was what the colonized were performing in.

Wole Soyinka's *Death and the King's Horsemen*, one of the greatest plays ever written on this subject, highlights this very phenomenon.

The play is based on real events during the Second World War when Nigeria was being ruled by the British. Elesin, the king's horseman according to the Yoruba, is to give up his life during the death ritual of the king. This is a performance that he has waited his entire life for. This is what his entire preparation and performance tradition is all about. However, at a banquet in a British official's house, Simon Pilkings, the colonial administrator, is notified that such an act is going to take place during his tenure. This practice has been banned by the British as a form of suicide and Pilkings must intervene on behalf of modernity.

An extraordinary challenge is thus set up in the play to our conventional ideas of modernity. Should Pilkings's action be about freedom and respect for other people's customs or about development, growth and against superstition? What happens when these positions are mutually exclusive? Such a clash is not uncommon even today world over in post-colonial societies.

Soyinka's greatness lies in the fact that not only does he manage to tell the story of the difference between two cultures but he also writes this play in their contrasting dramaturgical traditions of elaboration and compression. The first act containing the horseman's ritual is written in verse using extensive elaborations of mood and internal dialogue, whereas the second act is more in the world of traditional Western dramaturgy. I would imagine one would not only have to act differently in the two acts but also have to pause differently.

In modern times, this clash of performance traditions has compounded several times. The urban has not only bulldozed aspirations across rural traditions but also appropriated traditional dramaturgies into Western experiments. Indonesian dance performances, folk rituals from West Africa and Indian epic plays are all available at European festivals in sanitized formats. Condensed to shorter formats, placed under roving lights and on proscenium stages, these are the capsules that Western festivals and wealthy arts centres have paraded as the exotic and, worse still, as the 'genuine'. With no regard to the original context, these venues have managed to spawn an entire coterie of reviewers and academics who have given these venues their credibility. The worst kind of Orientalism meets the market in these sites of modern liberal art-making.

These commercial compromises are euphemistically called modernity and thus a permanent proselytization of audiences is at play. In several countries, I have met audiences who are avid theatre watchers but who believe that the theatre of the world is being preserved by such venues in the same way that British Petroleum believed for years that it was saving culture world over.

To bring art and theatre from traditional or rural dramaturgies lays an emphasis on the dramaturges of urbanity to translate it to their audiences. It is a neocolonial project to rest this responsibility on the marketing teams and then cut everything to the size of the attention span of the urban subject.

This contest between the two dramaturgies is going to be won hands down by the wealthier group. It is not surprising hence that in five-star hotels in Kerala we see Kathakali and Koodiyattam in twenty-minute capsules over dinner. That great masters have to record seven-second commercials in order to survive.

However, this is not being practical. It is not the success of the culture of mechanical time: it is its failure. It is the failure to protect that which human beings have developed over potentially the greatest years of philosophical advancement in favour of a 'technological epoch'. It is a failure to compromise on these huge advancements at understanding the subjectivities of human condition in order to fit into a template of urban internationalism.

And like every other period in human history when a culture has destroyed the basis of another, we know it is only the precursor to greater and more immediate tyrannies. The eradication of Jewish culture in Germany, the obliteration of art forms of the colonized and the annihilation of the tools and religions of the indigenous people – all led to massive unrests and evils in the world.

The way we treat time in our theatres today, and how we resolve this urban-rural tension in dramaturgy, is a precursor to what might come if we do not see the signs this time around. Oppression is always slow to come by. It does not have high velocity but continuous acceleration. It often starts with destroying the other's symbols, language, culture slowly. Then one day, it occupies centre stage with such force that it takes great human cost to overthrow it.

And at the heart of these beginnings is the fundamental unit of human understanding. The destruction of the other's concept of time. And I firmly believe it is up to art institutions to celebrate the diversity of different conceptions of time in their programming than to annihilate the differences in the name of efficiency.

There is no denying that the nature of Aristotelian treatment of time, although extremely useful to know, has become in today's European and American theatre a dogma. Anything that goes beyond that successfully is a successful experiment but not the given. Consequently, conversations with literary departments, dramaturgical teams and theatre managers who programme plays are replete with the same notion of a 'good play' being that which adheres to Aristotelian sense of time and where *exposition* is a bad word and *elaboration* boredom.

However, a dramatist in my view is essentially sculpting gaps of time. It is related to how we want our audience to reflect and what are the terms of engagement with the audience moment by moment as we set up the world of the play.

Time structure, or how we order time, is a cultural phenomenon. And if we want to engage with the world through our theatre, we have to bear the discomfort of engaging with plays and performances with different treatments of time, instead of wanting to fit everything into one idea of a 'good play' that has been defined by theatre buildings and newspapers for simplistic reasons rather than having any serious basis in a valid dramatic reason.

III

Any device of storytelling in a play that deals with time has a length. A line has a length; a pause has a length. An emotion, a moment of action, a song, an entry, a reveal, a distraction everything has a length.

Between these lengths of activities is the gap that will tell us what are the expectations in the room. The gap too has a length.

A meaningful moment on stage is one that has a meaningful gap between two actions. This is more or less a universal idea in theatre traditions world over, from Koodiyattam, Noh, Butoh, Kathakali to the dramatic writing of Chekhov, Pinter or Beckett.

'Time' in the theatre is experienced as much by the experience of these gaps as by the action.

The 'pause' is potentially one of the most powerful tools of a play.

In the European tradition of playwriting, Samuel Beckett has used gaps of duration to great effect in his plays. His entire oeuvre is essentially the choreography between the words. In the writing of the stage instructions itself, he has provided the rhythm in which the lines need to be performed. Hence, the durational gaps are written into the play, and as much as a night in theatre watching a Beckett play can be life-changing if these gaps are adhered to, it can be the worst night if they are not.

In Noh and Butoh, the duration of a sequence is critical to the storytelling, both dramatically and philosophically. The Japanese playwright Ōta Shōgo in his outstanding play *The Water Station* specifically instructs that two metres of stage length should be covered in no less than five minutes.

The Water Station is a play with no dialogue but a detailed written composition of movement. The text of *The Water Station* does not have dialogues but instead has actions.

In a sense, Beckett and Shōgo are coming from the same place. They are both masters of creating meaningful gaps in the activity in our mind which allows us to understand the conditions of the character as much as the plot.

IV

Some years ago, I had the opportunity to see the production of *The Great Gatsby* by a New York-based company, Elevator Repair Service. In this production, the entire book by Fitzgerald is read. Every single line. The play lasts for nine hours with two breaks in between, and the only way this text is delivered is not by rushing it but in fact by taking one's time.

One of the tools that is used for this is that of repetition. From the beginning, the soundscape is filled with repetition, and every time a door opens or shuts in the office where they work, one hears a repetitive motif.

This immediately does two things.

One, it tells us that life repeats. Things reappear. Mundanity is part of the picture.

And within this mundanity extraordinary things happen.

Two, it gives us form. The form develops slowly, but over time we learn how to watch this work. Its intricate layers, the fine lattice work that is hidden behind the outer structure of its shape.

The dramatists of Elevator Repair Service pepper their production text with a number of repetitions of different kinds in order to deliver a formal achievement of the highest order.

For days it reminded me of Kathakali and how form develops in Kathakali. Kathakali which often deals with stories of *Mahabharata*.

Every character who enters has a section of elaboration of their own character and then their premise. Once again here, we see several repetitions of facial expressions, colours of masks, forms of speech that are distinctly repeated by specific characters in order to take us towards the plot's conflict.

Thinking about the similarities between the nine-hour production of *The Great Gatsby* by Elevator Repair Service and Kathakali Productions, I learnt one of the most important lessons about the theatre. *That a play that stays with us often does so as much through its pauses as it does through its lines or actions.*

We remember Hamlet's 'To be or not to be' in terms of both what was said and how it was paused.

Paul Goodman in his book *Speaking and Language: Defence of Poetry* beautifully outlines nine kinds of silence.

Goodman writes:

> Not speaking and speaking are both human ways of being in the world, and there are kinds and grades of each. There is the dumb silence of slumber or apathy; the sober silence that goes with a solemn animal face; the fertile silence of awareness, pasturing the soul, whence emerge new thoughts; the alive silence of alert perception, ready to say, 'This . . . this . . .'; the musical silence that accompanies absorbed activity; the silence of listening to another speak, catching the drift and helping him be clear; the noisy silence of resentment and self-recrimination, loud and subvocal speech but sullen to say it; baffled silence; the silence

of peaceful accord with other persons or communion with the cosmos.

In an evening of good theatre anywhere in the world, one experiences not only an exciting range of ideas and emotions but also a musical score of the most profound pauses.

My teacher Thomas Prattki used to say in class, 'There are two situations when we do not use words in a relationship. One, when there are no words as yet, and two, when there is nothing left to be said.'

I think this relationship extends not only between the characters but also between the dramatist and the audience in the theatre. This relationship of silence perhaps holds more uniformity across cultures, from Ouagadougou to the West End in London, than any predefined definition of what makes a good play or the ideal arrangement of time.

And if we are interested in truly international work, we must understand the way a culture pauses in order to appreciate its theatre.

While I was developing *Pah-la*, the play on contemporary Tibet and the future of non-violent struggles, I was extensively involved in researching Tibetan Buddhist performance traditions.

One evening in Shillong, a hill station in North-East India, I was at a Buddhist monastery which was about to host a performance. It was a special day according to the Buddhist calendar and the play was as much a ritual as a performance for entertainment.

In fact, my wife, Pallavi, and I had gone to see something else in the hills when we were told that the monastery was going to have a performance that evening. We walked in and found people sitting in the courtyard. The performance had already started and some of the characters in masks were playing with young children in the audience. This participatory mode is intrinsic to Buddhist performance. On one side of the monastery was a door from which the characters were going to emerge. They were to pass through the courtyard and go to a tent on the opposite side where they would sit next to the monks and musicians on normal chairs.

After some time, the music started to play and the doors opened. Gods appeared. Demons appeared. There was no fourth wall, but there were five dimensions. Length, breadth, depth, height and infinite time. Time measured in the silences the characters held. In how they walked towards the tent and in no time became gods from humans and humans from gods. They moved from the silence of the gods to the silence of the humans.

During all this, the sun began to set.

We could all see the sun hanging in the sky above the mountain to our west. The pipes were playing, the drums were beating and the actors were moving.

Then for a moment everything paused. The sound, the action and the audience's body changed. Everyone held that pause. The bright orange sun paused for a moment, and it was one of the most perfect pauses I have ever encountered anywhere.

Humans, Gods, Music, Action and the Sun had paused on top of the Himalayas.

We breathed together. The Sun set.

The play continued.

That moment cannot be recreated in a theatre building.

That pause is unavailable outside that dramaturgy.

11

On censorship

I

The voice

It was early morning. Perhaps 4.00 am. I was about to get up from bed and start working on a new draft of a play. The previous evening, I had collated all my notes. The references had been written down in my diary. The pictures that are relevant to this play were neatly arranged in a folder on my desktop and the physical copies, in a large envelope made out of newspaper. I had filled ink in my fountain pen. All routine checks had been done before I went to bed. While working on a new play, I usually wake up at 4.00 am and write till about 7.00 am before taking a short nap again. These morning hours have traditionally been my best hours for new writing. During the day, I generally revise, read and work on my direction projects.

My three-year-old daughter was holding me and sleeping. I removed her hand from my body, got out of the bed and placed a pillow in my place so that she doesn't fall down from my side of the bed. She held the pillow as if she recognized that it was not me. She shuffled a little and held it again as if aware of the compromises she has to make for her father's art. I smiled looking at her.

I got up. Got myself a cup of tea and sat at my desk in the bedroom. I switched on the table lamp and was about to get started.

I put pen to paper and was about to write the first stage directions of my play *Baatin*, when suddenly for the first time in my life I sat paralysed. This play set on the night of the death of the Prophet Muhammad (PBUH) is about Quranic exegesis. About the exploration of the Inner (*baatin*) meaning of the Quran versus its Outer (*zaahir*) meaning. I had researched it for over a year and a half across Islamic schools and in conversation with scholars around the world. I knew where to begin in this new draft and yet I sat still unable to know how to start.

For the first time in my life, other than my family, my characters and me, there was another person in the room. I wanted to write what I felt, but a voice in my head had appeared from somewhere. It kept telling me, 'If you do not change yourself, your life as a playwright is over. No one will ever know that you exist. Your plays will not see the light of day. Don't write this character. Don't make him say what you are thinking of. If you don't change yourself . . .' In a loop.

I had never faced writer's block in my life. Never faced the problem of staring at a blank page and not knowing where to begin. I had always managed to start by starting. And once I got started, I worked it out, draft after draft. That's it. That had been my formula. Prepare. Draft. Read. Revise. Over and over again, till I was convinced about where it got to. No intimidation by goons, police or government agencies had stopped me from writing what I wanted to, and I had had the privilege of working with people who had never asked me to compromise. I had managed to keep my work insulated from all voices that would compromise its quality or intent. But this morning, I sat paralysed. The censor had entered my head. It had developed my vocabulary and my expressions. I sat at my desk helplessly. There was no else to fight this time except myself. And I knew that this would be the toughest censor to fight. Finally, I had internalized that which I had wholeheartedly opposed for years before this morning.

II

The year of censorship

The first half of 2019 had been surreal. We staged the Hindustani version of *Djinns of Eidgah* in Jaipur in North India, and after one show, it was shut down by the police. A right-wing Hindu group had filed a police complaint against it, calling it seditious and insulting to India. The play had been booked under the draconian censorship law, the Theatre Censorship Act of 1876, and had been stopped from getting staged.

A few months later, I went to London for the opening of *Pahla* at the Royal Court Theatre and all hell broke loose. I had to decline multiple offers by Chinese agents to sell the play to them with a contract that would effectively ensure the play was never staged. After repeated offers and then threats, when it was clear that I was not selling it, there was a last-ditch effort to negotiate to make certain changes to the text. I had gotten into a fight, bust my right eye, torn a muscle and a small play-reading in Lhasa had led to arrests.

On the other hand, a small group of Tibetans ran an active campaign online to defame the production. Two out of five of them had auditioned for it and not made it through. At least on three counts, what they objected to as misrepresentation were the same sections which the Chinese authorities wanted to change!

The play eventually ran successfully and the head of the Tibetan Community in the UK publicly felicitated the actors and director on the last day of the show. His Holiness the Dalai Lama's representative in the UK saw the play twice and congratulated the team. However, on social media, we faced false accusations day in and day out from this small group.

The play by now has been translated to Tibetan and has a multi-country tour in 2022–3, but at that time it was being censored from both the Chinese agents and this small group of Tibetans who were offended by the Tibetan violence in the play.

I was thus aware that essentially two of the major plays I had worked on in the last decade were censored or shut down by Chinese and Indian authorities who otherwise are at loggerheads with each other. I went to teach playwriting at NYU Abu Dhabi knowing very well that although I was nurturing young playwrights, nothing I had written in the last few years was going to be allowed on stage anytime soon. The thought was crippling. It was a dead end.

Some people had suggested that I should write something else. About subjects that were non-controversial. Curiously, they didn't understand that I wasn't writing 'controversial' plays; I was writing what I could. To change my writing, my entire life would have to change. I would have to be born in a different family, go to a different school, read other books, love other people, have other friends, marry someone else and have a different child. I was not being brave, purposeful, important or immediate. I was being myself.

And that is the first and foremost important challenge as a writer when it comes to facing censorship. Censors are not asking us to change our vocation. They are asking us to change our history. They are not asking us to erase a line. They are asking us to erase our bedtime stories. They are not here to change our opportunities, they are here to change the voice inside our heads.

And it is the job of every self-respecting artist in the world today to fight wholeheartedly for their own voice. There are many ways in which this voice can be compromised. Some methods are clearer than others and hence, easier to oppose. Other methods are important to spot and harder to oppose.

III

Good censors, bad censors

Bad censors are old-fashioned. They are loud, direct, morally and intellectually untenable. The people who stopped *Djinns of Eidgah* from playing in Jaipur were such people. Although in the immediate sense they manage to threaten people and get their work stopped, their censorship does not have long-term repercussions. On the contrary, in many ways they elevate the status of the artist by giving them this kind of attention. Unless, of course, they shoot the artist dead, which is an abhorrent act like no other.

The good censor, however, is the harder one to counter. Worldwide the long-lasting censors of art at the highest and most prevalent level have been censors of this kind who appear completely committed to the greater common good but are detrimental to the act of questioning. The good censor is the essential neoliberal whose limits of tolerance extend only to incorporate regime, capital and art that is friendly to the status quo. This censor engages in methods such as buying out dissenters and artists, failing at which leads them to ban, boycott, conduct media trials of the artist's work and personal choices, thereby making it impossible for the artist's work to be produced.

One of the best examples of this that I have ever encountered is from Burkina Faso, told to me by my friend and theatre artist Ildevert who practises in Ouagadougou, the capital. We were sitting one night with another artist, Sinaray, at a small beer-and-food shop when Sinaray mentioned his first ordeal with political ramifications of their work.

The event occurred around 1988 after their revolutionary hero Thomas Sankara had been assassinated by his own comrade Blaise Compaoré. Thomas Sankara was responsible for freeing Burkina Faso from colonial French rule. Sankara had also been the first president of a free Burkina Faso. Compaoré had taken over the presidentship through a coup d'etat against Sankara and stayed in power from 1987 to 2014. In 2014, he was ousted by a popular uprising by the people. Compaoré had had Sankara assassinated and then buried with presidential guards watching over the grave. People were not even allowed to see his last remains, let alone get close to them.

A few months later, Sinaray's theatre group was performing *Antigone*. Burkina Faso has a robust and thriving theatre culture and Sankara himself was a champion of the theatre. Even today, despite the poverty in the country, there are several theatres across the cities.

The *Antigone* production was doing very well and was much talked about. People were flocking in to see it, and one evening, the new dictator decided to be in the audience himself with his presidential guards. Within the first ten minutes, the moment it was established that Antigone had been denied the opportunity to bury the dead bodies of her brothers by Creon, the tension in the theatre was palpable. Apparently, people in the theatre were so terrified of how the dictator would respond that no one applauded even the best speeches and dialogues that otherwise were applauded every day. After the show, Sinaray and his colleagues were trembling in the green room anticipating what Compaoré would do to them. They had started to rehearse this play even before Sankara was killed, and it was more of a political reflection on that time as opposed to a comment on any one incident. Suddenly, a group of presidential guards walked into the green room and asked the actors to come on stage. The actors were so sure that they were going to be shot dead in public that some of them wet their pants on the summon.

On stage, Compaoré greeted each one of them. He congratulated them in front of the audience for the play and added sternly that they must make responsible art that helps society rather than one which spreads rumours. Sinaray said that just that much was enough to threaten us. Till the dictator left the theatre building, no one was sure if they were going to live or die through that evening.

After telling me this story, when Sinaray left us, Ildevert told me, 'But he hasn't told you the whole story. How did Compaoré make sure that they never made such theatre again?'

'How?' I asked.

'He gave them a building, salaries, equipment and made them the national theatre. Once they had everything they needed to make good theatre, they could never question the government again.'

This kind of censorship is an extremely important phenomenon that Ildevert illuminated for me. Since then I have seen and noticed this way of censorship in many places in the world. And I am convinced that every artist and society have to fight this kind of censorship most actively; in fact, this is the harder one to fight.

To counter censorship is also to counter the censorship of large institutions, governments and festivals if they trade opportunity with freedom of speech. An extremely wealthy private festival in India once asked me to make a new work for them for a lot of money provided the work had no 'religion, politics or sexuality'. Of course, what they mean by this is that the work should not question established norms on these subjects rather than not having them altogether. Obviously, I had to decline.

This has been the pattern in India with major government institutions as well. If one does not tow the government line in their politics, national festivals discard the artist, messages are sent to repertories and groups performing the artist's work to stop these performances, government grants to them are blocked if they do not comply.

The erstwhile soft power of money is now the hard power. Or it could be that this has been some ancient truth. I had read that during the period of the great Greek plays, there were play competitions in which tragedies had a greater prize money than comedies. This is why there are more tragedies than comedies.

I am not sure if this is true, but it certainly is true of our times. Culture is not being administered but created by the powers.

The rise of the far-right in several parts of the world after the global economic crash of 2008–9 and the rise of insular capitalism are inextricably linked. The incentives to both are exclusivist and financial but under the garb of the greater common good of protecting local interests.

I have received death threats thrice so far. However, they never bothered me. I did not come to the theatre to please people. I am not leaving if someone wants me to. They should have no other choice but to wish that I would die if they wanted me to not make what I do.

What bothers me is the 'good censor'. One who censors art and makes the act look benevolent. Who runs the market and then cites 'market forces' to promote, create and support regressive ideas in society.

The good censor garbs regression in the garb of sponsorship, awards and, in extreme cases, under the illusion of an abstract idea of survival. Any artist who needs to compromise on the content of their art to survive should remember that from then on, they lose the right to call themselves an artist. There is no such thing as half-art. Either one goes all the way or one does not. In villages, fishing communities, labour movements and tribal cultures, I have never seen anyone have the dilemma of good art versus a good life. It is only in the middle class that aspiration and art clash.

While making *Pah-la*, I knew it would not be easy to thwart Chinese attempts at censorship. But I did not want them to get by as good censors. In a way, their defeat was in the fact that they had to bust my eye and become goons.

IV

Historical imperative

Queen Victoria took over as empress of India from the British East India Company in 1876. One of the first laws she introduced was the Dramatic Censorship Act of 1876 with the 'power to prohibit certain dramatic performances . . . of a scandalous or defamatory nature, or likely to excite feelings of disaffection to the Government established by the law in [British] India'.

This act was created first and foremost to censor a Bangla play called *Neel Darpan*, or Indigo Mirror. The play was about the exploitation of the indigo plantation workers. When it was staged on a plantation, some of the workers got up on stage and started beating up the actor playing the English officer when he kicked a worker. We should remind ourselves that the workers in real life were kicked and beaten regularly but never protested. They accepted this as their condition. However, once they had the distance of an audience, they could not hold themselves back. The commentators of that time had gone on print saying that the workers were illiterate and did not understand the theatre.

When the play was staged for British officers they attacked the actors too. This time it was a scene where the British officers were mocked. They were literate.

The Queen and her advisors were smart enough to realize that after the First War of Independence of 1857, there were many sore wounds among the British officers and population. Although the British had managed to retain India after killing thousands of Indians, the damage inflicted on the lives of British soldiers was also considerable. This was not the time for a play that depicted the poor conditions of plantation workers working under British officers. This was time for hollow nationalism and empire-building.

We should take note of the fact that even today in Waterloo Place stands the statue of Colin Campbell, or Lord Clyde. In his epitaph, Lord Clyde is hailed for 'fifty years of arduous service' culminating in the 'pacification of India in 1858'. Even today, nowhere in his epitaph or his statue it is mentioned that it was the First War of Independence by the colonial subjects of India and Lord Clyde was the commander-in-chief of the Imperial Army that killed thousands of people to deny them their right to self-rule. I do not mean to have a trial for Lord Clyde anachronistically. However, it is baffling to me that even today such an act of censorship of history stands with such grandeur at an iconic site and hundreds of people go there every month and click pictures with his statue at the back.

Coming back to the censorship act, let us also note that live performances world over have been one of the first forms to be stopped or appropriated by colonizers of all kinds. When Lorca was shot dead as capital punishment, it is said that the first person to have fired a shot was a die-hard Lorca fan. Nationalism and religious dogma can blind us to our taste and sensibilities to this extent. There is an unusual power in a person saying something in flesh and blood in front of a society, questioning its assumptions. Society is a malleable, nebulous entity. Greek tragedy shows us that one person stepping out of the chorus can bring down an emperor.

The historical imperative to censor rests eternally with the ruler and the historical imperative to oppose it with the artist. This contest is three way. There are gods, rulers and artists. Each vying for the mind-space of the audience. Gods and rulers never give up their side of the rope. Neither should artists.

Whenever I am asked by someone 'What is theatre good for?' or 'Does it really make a difference in the world?' I always say I do not know. But ask the government. Ask the institutions that ban plays. Ask big corporations that spend millions of dollars on promoting celebratory fairy tales with moderate social dilemmas in their characters. They definitely seem to believe that two people on stage in a tiny theatre somewhere that is half-full on a Sunday afternoon can change the world.

The power of theatre is unknown to the artist. It is known to the censor.

V

The case for censorship

In 2015, when I went to China and read the daily English papers in my hotel, it struck me that there is no bad news in China. Day after day, other than natural calamities and the odd corrupt official who had already been arrested, there was really nothing to be sad or critical of in that large country. An hour's tour around Beijing would, however, belie this notion. What was also striking is that it always felt like capitalism outside China was about to collapse any day. I was terribly surprised to see that there were so many news reports of people's disgruntlement with capitalism. It seemed like every day America was on the brink of collapse and that China was forming new allies.

A year later, I was in New York City and in the so-called haven of free speech I started to read their English dailies. Needless to say, according to American media, China is about to collapse any day and every day America too is forming new allies with disgruntled Chinese communists who want to make the switch.

The point I want to make is not that both sides are lying or both are telling the truth. The point is that both are censoring the news in order to support the basis and beliefs of their society.

The focus on maintaining status quo is often referred to as the primary reason for there to be different types of censorship. Personal, institutional, economic, cultural and legal. I have been told multiple times that in a country like India we are not equipped to handle the discontent of a largely mixed and volatile population. That in China they cannot possibly be reading literature about immediate Tibetan grievances for the sake of a larger grand vision of the People's Republic. That Tibetans-in-exile cannot be told of the violent struggles inside Tibet as it is impossible for violence to exist in the freedom struggle purely because it should not exist. That in England, a major theatre cannot produce a play on the Quran because the Muslim community would apparently bring the theatre down if it disagrees in parts with the work.

The list is long and based on two elementarily flawed assumptions.

The first assumption is that people, irrespective of who they are, are homogenous and stupid. In none of the cases listed earlier, has there been any criticism or enquiry about the work itself being accurate or inaccurate, aesthetic or not, politically compelling or not. About the work reflecting a reality of the world or being a piece of propaganda. There is no contesting of the idea. No discussion on the history presented or the central thesis. No genuine reading. It is purely decision makers and people in power deciding that the work is too complex for common people and that it could lead to a homogenous unrest. The censorship is in place to avoid the inconvenience of having to argue with dissenting groups, of having to test and examine a work to see if it holds, to put in the effort to stand by ideas that challenge the existing axioms of social and political understanding.

The second fatal assumption is to believe that the artist's role is to bring people together. Isaiah Berlin, the philosopher, said that the role of a philosopher is to question the fundamental assumptions of society so that it moved forward. That society and civilization progress by doing a form of parricide where you do not kill your father but definitely kill the ideas of the fathers. Without the dynamism, there would be no progress at all and we would all be ossified.

Berlin goes on to say that not everyone of course should be doing this. If everyone in society continuously questioned everything all the time, there would be no forward movement of society in that case as well. The point is to let each role in society exist and play its role for the betterment of society.

This line of thinking extends to artists who are fundamentally 'philosophers of the people'. Our job is to conduct this parricide of ideas. Not without deep engagement. Not to sensationalize or create cheap and easy provocation. However, our job is also not to bring people together or make people blindly celebrate the structure in which we live. Our job is to make entertainment a civilizational virtue and not a civilizational distraction.

This is why artists should not bother about censorship while creating the work. Censorship is a bogus, arrogant self-important activity that is all about going around the world posturing caution in art, claiming that its receivers are incapable of handling the challenges to existing norms. Art has survived for the opposite reason as religion. Religion is here to give answers to questions like 'Why are we here?'. Art is here to ask the question, 'What kind of "why" are we asking in why are we here?' Is it the same kind of 'why' that we ask in an empirical realm, such as 'Why does it rain?' Or is it another kind of abstract 'why', whose real focus lies in some other human need? Art is about the deeper questions that drive us and not about the kind of simple solutions that religion provides for these questions.

This is why artists throughout history have opposed censorship. It may have its costs but that is really the job at hand.

VI

Two painters in Prague

In Prague's Old Town Square stands a studio. In 2009, when I was there, there were two painters who worked in the studio. They had both been practising in Hungary earlier and had suffered under the communist regime. There were severe restrictions to what kind of art could be produced, and they found it extremely stifling. When the

Berlin Wall was brought down, they moved to Prague. Communism had come apart and here was an opportunity to create art freely.

They set up this studio and the two of them shared the rent. They painted through the day and tried to sell some pieces to tourists in order to make a living. Business was not picking up as quickly as they expected.

One of them created a tiny string puppet one day. Just for fun, he started to paint by manipulating the hands of this puppet. People started to trickle in to his side of the studio and business started to pick up a little. On gauging that this was a potentially successful business idea he made a giant puppet. Life size. Making it to the Guinness World Records as the world's largest puppet-painter. Business started to boom for him.

The man who told me this story was the painter without the puppet. Outside their studio was a big board which had a picture of the puppet declaring its Guinness feat. Inside was the painter and his friend's puppet on the other side.

The walls were filled with beautiful paintings made by this painter and a few terrible ones made by the puppet that still sold much faster than the former. People bought them in order to see the puppet make them. These were just samples.

When I asked him where his friend was, he said that the friend had already gone home. He only worked five hours as opposed to this man who worked till late. His friend made money by painting for tourists within a few hours while he stayed in the studio longer.

'Why doesn't he paint his own work after?' I asked.

'He can't,' the man replied. 'He's lost the joy in painting. He makes his money, goes home and drinks. He hates painting.'

Communism had thwarted his creativity. Capitalism had destroyed his being.

VII

Re-finding one's voice

I was fortunate to recognize that this new voice was not mine. I struggled with it for a few days but never seriously considered making peace with it. I fought and kept writing what I wanted to but it occupied the kind of attention that a writer cannot give to anyone else while writing.

This went on for a month or so. But I did what I do whenever I am faced with a block in my work. I just work more.

So, I immersed myself in rehearsals as a director, in running our company, in writing new scenes and teaching classes. I also read a lot of work by the Lebanese novelist Elias Khoury.

Many voices started to enter my mind. Voices of collaborators, stage managers, actors and of course Khoury.

I stopped talking to the press altogether. Took no calls to explain myself about the two plays that had been banned.

One morning at 4.00 am, I found myself copying Khoury in my style of writing. As I copied him, the voice of doubt in my head began to fade. I remembered that a few years ago I had heard him in a talk, and he said that the greatest award he ever received was that for a few days a free Palestinian camp was set up in a liberated area, and it was named after his novel *Gate of the Sun*. I wondered if anyone else has ever had that honour. A country finally frees itself for a few days and it names itself over a writer's novel.

His works too had been banned.

In about a week, I realized his voice was fading. Suddenly, I had mine back. The master had cleansed my mind of the shock of being met with such strong opposition. First, he had killed their voices in my head, and then, his own.

I was well on my way to writing *Baatin*. The voices of my collaborators and heroes had trumped the voices of my censors.

12

The pandemic and the theatre

I

When I started writing this book, the greatest impediment to it was travel. Every month, on an average, I travelled for about ten days with one performance or the other. In months that I did not travel for shows, I was out of home, either rehearsing or teaching somewhere else in the world.

Some of the early chapters in this book were written in Dubai, London, New York and on flights between several Indian cities. This despite wanting to wholeheartedly avoid writing outside of my homes in Bangalore and Abu Dhabi.

In early 2020, the pandemic hit the world. In March 2020, we had the first lockdown in India and now it is July 2021. In nearly a year and a half, this book has had no reason to be written anywhere else. These sixteen months are the longest period in the last sixteen years that I have not travelled for a play. It is ironic that a book called *Theatre Across Borders* ends with a chapter which is written at a time when most borders in the world are completely sealed.

In some way, it also seems like the perfect ending. Because now one is forced to ask what was that 'normal' we the theatre fraternity were in, what is the crisis, how did we respond to it, what good are the arts in times of such a crisis and will there be a new normal?

II

What was our 'normal'?

The first thing to acknowledge is that although we are in a global pandemic, the virus affects everyone differently. The reality of this pandemic is that its primary virus has spread itself around the world through the rich and its most long-lasting effects will be seen by the poor.

The coronavirus has effectively made it impossible to hide the disparities of the world. If anything, it has further illuminated something we knew all along: that in our world, there is abhorrent inequality in terms of opportunity, standard of life, security, access to health care, education and domestic well-being. The virus has made it impossible for us to keep our pretensions about these inequalities alive.

We – the privileged of the world who have access to food, housing, clothing and education – can no longer pretend that life will go on as usual and the 'system' will take care of those who do not have these essentials. The cost of our apathy is no longer a normalized sense of violence among the dispossessed. The cost now is death, disease, hunger and domestic violence. Our structures of society and the design of our cities have been exposed during the pandemic to reveal the multiple forms of apartheid that still exist in the world. The virus has shown us that we do not have infinite time to solve the crisis of inequality.

My office in India is an apartment with two study rooms, about a twenty-minute drive from my house. I work alone out of that office all day. In that locality itself, petty crime and theft have gone up by 25 per cent in the last two months of staggered lockdown. People who have nothing to eat and no source of income are left with no other choice but to steal from those of us who continue to lead their lives as if this was a long holiday. A holiday from where we worked from home and learnt to bake new cakes, as opposed to those who starved indoors.

Starved, because they have no place in this world unless they step out and do the manual work of this world.

We must remember that this inequality and stark difference are not something that the pandemic has created. This was our normal.

The French economist Thomas Piketty in his book *Capital and Ideology* shows us that although the overall wealth of the world has increased in the last centuries, inequality in the last century has risen by multiple times across continents. The historically low wealth-tax rates that operate currently in the world, compared to post-war rates, show us clearly that the argument for individual wealth being drivers of larger good holds no water. Just after the war, as nations were rebuilding, the United States, for instance, had a wealth tax of 60 per cent compared to now when it is close to 30 per cent. At that time, world economies saw the maximum growth in overall terms through industrialization and modernization of post-war countries.

In fact, worldwide we see this phenomenon of disproportionate rise of wealth and abhorrently low rates of wealth tax. In India, during the pandemic itself, as millions of people were displaced, starved and killed due to lack of basic housing or health care, the wealth of the top 2 per cent rose by 35 per cent. India created several new billionaires during the months of the pandemic.

When the second wave was about to hit India, a day before lockdown, seventy super-rich families of India booked chartered planes and flew to London. They are people who hold more than 50 per cent of the Indian economy. The rest of the country was left to die here. So many people died due to lack of oxygen that in North India people were cremated by the roadside. Lakhs of people died without their families by their side. They were just collected in heaps by generous frontline workers and burnt. The air smelt of burning flesh. The sky was full of soot.

This dramatic image of burning will forever be an image of the pandemic etched in my mind. These people did not die because they contracted the virus. They died because there were no beds and no oxygen for them. They died because they do not exist in the imagination of this world. Because their stories do not make it to the main stages of the theatre or the big screen of the cinema. They are subjects of documentary films. Their value in the media rests on the extremities of their suffering.

This was the normal within which we were all creating work before the pandemic. We had internalized inequality and we thought intrinsically it was normal. Steps to equity were considered idealistic but not urgent. This reflected too in our own theatre buildings, their programming, casting and recruitment of creative leaders.

The second acknowledgement we need to make is that before the pandemic we had all internalized a fundamental agreement to the structure of free-market economy. We had also assumed that whether we liked it or not, we are bound to participate in the story of infinite growth. That competence, hard work and talent are the only qualities that will make one do well in life. That ultimately, since communism has supposedly collapsed, the only possibility in our lives is to participate in the idea that if everyone optimizes their gain, the system will gain overall. That competition invariably leads to efficient systems.

Today, we are at a place where all our rags-to-riches stories fail us. We are Cinderella and it is a perpetual 12 o'clock. Any moment our shoes can vanish. Our reality can be revealed. The spell of infinite growth is over.

Adam Smith, who presented the free-market idea in one of its earliest forms, is often quoted from his book *Wealth of Nations* about the importance of the 'invisible hand'. The invisible hand is said to drive free markets to greater efficiencies and better profits for everyone. The proponents of this kind of market structure often fail to pick up another passage in the same book where Smith cautions about 'the invisible fist' accompanying the invisible hand.

The invisible fist is the fist of control, power, authority and unfair trade practices that do not allow equity. We live in a world where a myth has been created that state subsidy is something lazy people receive, who by virtue of their lack of enterprise are also poor. As if the subsidy is not coming from a historical understanding of rights but from the purse of a strict father.

In the theatre, this belief in the invisible hand without acknowledging the invisible fist turned out to be one of its first nemesis the moment the pandemic erupted. There were hardly any institutions around the world that could save theatre-makers across forms, artists, technicians, managers, administrative staff and teachers from a life of hardship and uncertainty. Isn't it baffling that an art form that has been intrinsic to human beings for three thousand years has to ask itself if it is relevant during a pandemic? Is that the right question? Is chess relevant? Is music relevant during war? Is having children, falling in love, grieving over dead people, looking at stars and wondering what lies beyond relevant in times of epidemics?

The point I want to make is that this question about relevance is a false one. Something does not have to be top priority all the time for it to be relevant all the time. Our lives are replete with multiple objects of experience. Their utility is not always the same. However, they are what make us who we are.

How can we as a society behave as if after the pandemic being human itself will not include the arts? The billionaires who left India just before the lockdown, the billionaires of Brazil, the billionaires of Silicon Valley, have all earned their money sitting on millions of dollars of subsidies, tax holidays and infrastructural support provided by the hard-earned money of common people. When the pandemic struck us, we were as a world stuck within a worldview of such tacit belief in the free market that we never asked whether chartered jets, luxury cars, landholding of islands and concentration of 70 per cent of the world's wealth in the pockets of 7 per cent were a luxury. We were only asking if the school teacher, the theatre artist and the folk singer were a luxury to society. Our normal before the pandemic included the false belief that the invisible hand will be for the greater common good of all and meritocracy shall see us through hard times. We consciously did not prioritize the idea that true meritocracy needs to be judged by looking at the starting point for everyone and not by examining the rate of growth of a few individuals. The unquestioning belief in free market itself was a flaw in our normal. Today we are in a world where everyone can die if one person has the virus and yet the formula for the vaccine is not in public domain. People know that with adequate profits it is possible to create an alternate world where the diseases of the common people do not reach those above them. We, the theatre-makers, had ourselves internalized the false premise of the invisible hand so deeply that our own systems did not make the question of 'Why is theatre relevant?' obsolete. We tried to answer this false question repeatedly on multiple forums.

The third big flaw with our normal included completely bogus categories of identity. We spent too much time being precious about our own cultures as if our cultures were implicitly coded in our genes. Even the curiosity for other cultures was fundamentally entrenched in the self-righteousness of curiosity for the 'other'.

After the financial crisis of 2007–8, as the pipe dream of international capital began to fade, people voted for hard-line nationalist governments. India, Brazil, Turkey, Hungary, the United States, France, Indonesia, Italy and many more countries have voted for the right wing or centrist-right in the elections after 2008.

The fear comes from the idea that the liberals have gone ahead and exposed us to the entire world's risk in a global economic framework. If something happens in Manhattan, there are food-riots in Egypt.

This point, however, still remains. Hard-line nationalist governments worldwide have sold out and divested profit-making public-sector companies in all these countries to global corporations. Everyone is sitting with seventeen brands of cereals from three companies on their racks.

However, what we have all bought into is the myth of singular identity. The right wing identifies itself in strict insular boxes that are watertight and the liberals identify themselves in the same insular boxes, only with some translucent windows and a good dose of guilt. So, everyone is reduced to being Indian, Japanese, British as a primary identifier. Around the world, too many theatres and cultural institutions have identified artists exclusively by their nationality and nothing else. They have been expected to tell their stories and their stories alone. In the pretext of guilt, cultures and countries that have no reason not to write about each other have been sent on a predisposed exile wherein their young have to ask themselves 'Can I write about another place?' As if people do not belong to socio-economic classes. As if the rich in Manhattan have more in common with the poor in Queens or Harlem than the rich in Mumbai. As if the history of Asia with its multiple travellers writing each other's anthropology from the seventh century does not exist, as if history begins with the white man arriving on a boat.

These false categories were paraded in false divisions such as the international festival, the Global South meeting, the MENASA countries meet, the African diaspora theatre festival and so on.

The truth is that once we have truly integrated the world in our thought, we do not need these categories. We can programme our lives, our theatre, our politics by the real sense of identity which is, in fact, a mixed bag of multiple identities.

The pandemic has demolished these identities. It has clearly pointed out that during a crisis the most pervasive category is wealth. The rich of poorer countries are safer from the virus than the poor of richer countries. Period. All nuances are inside these categories thereafter.

Our belief in these identities was so strict and strong that not only did we have an unquestioned unequal world, but we also believed that the world is genuinely populated by 180 species that live in 180 countries. All our frames of negotiation – from climate, to oil to theatre – came from this frame.

When the first lockdown happened in India, I was out every day with a volunteer group distributing ration in slums in our neighbourhood. It started as a small exercise for three to five families whose children study in a free school for underprivileged children that I am a part of. In three months, we had thirteen thousand people across three thousand families on our list. Many of these families lived in clusters in these slums. When we went into these areas, often houses were clustered by region. Some clusters claimed they were local to the state. Some others claimed that they were local to the city, and hence, the people who were local only to the state are actually outsiders to the city. Then, there were those who were migrant workers from other states, who in turn had within them sub-clusters from different states.

By the end of the first month, I realized that the government had not provided anyone adequate food for their families and everyone was starving. However, everyone believed that the other group had received the ration, and it was because of the other that these people are not getting the food. We had to keep asking people to question the government and not each other.

I would come home and interact with theatres and institutions worldwide, many of whom I was working with but had now gone into lockdown. The conversations obviously veered towards a complete loss of how to go on without opening the theatre. But also, about which identity should be programmed. Should it be local writers, South Asian, Latin, African, MENASA, European, white American or some other category that would need the focus once theatres opened.

Here we were, in the middle of the biggest pandemic since the Spanish flu, indiscriminately dying. Our social and economic conditions were exposing us to different kinds of threats and health care. And our work was still trying to figure out if we were the right region.

It is part of our pre-pandemic normal to think of the world as a conglomeration of singular identities. This leads us to feel superior to everyone else, and then we carry our distorted view of this planet into the theatre and commission work inside it depending on who is from where and who should create what kind of work.

III

What is the crisis, and how did we respond?

Death is the most immediate end we are all trying to avoid. However, the will to fight death is intrinsic to all animals. All of us want to live and anything that threatens our lives or the lives of our loved ones is met with our complete attention.

As a civilization, the human race has thrived due to its peculiar mastery over nature. The way we have controlled nearly every aspect of this planet is hugely responsible for our phenomenal success as a species. We have in our short history not only managed to track nearly all animals but continue to control most of their lives at our will. We have managed to get to the bottom of the oceans, to the tips of the planets and most recently conducted experiments on Mars. No other species of animals can claim to come even close to this kind of success at leaving its mark on all aspects of a planet.

However, civilization is not made up of our significant achievements. Civilization is a process, not a destination. And today, as we are brought to our knees by a tiny virus, we need to examine our civilization deeply. We are able to study the moon but we cannot ensure that everyone who is out of work right now gets to eat three square meals. Nations and corporations who can ensure that every child in the world has access to Coca-Cola cannot ensure that every child has milk. The pandemic, from where I am, is a mirror to show us how undignified we have made the lives of so many people. But at the heart of it, I believe, the crisis, at least in India and similarly in most of the world's poor and populous countries, was not about death but about dignity.

When my friend and I went on our food support initiative, we would see people standing close to the van and not voluntarily walk up to receive the ration kits. They would not ask for food. Till a few days ago, all of them were employed, either in permanent jobs or as daily-wage labour. They had left their villages to come to the city in order to live a life of dignity. They never wanted to ask for food. However, now they were reduced to doing just that. We had to invite them to take the food kits. We had to tell them it was their right.

It was an endless cycle of food requests after that. My phone would buzz from 9.00 am in the morning to about midnight, and we had multiple vans going all around Bangalore doing this work. The most important part of this was not the food distribution or raising money for this but to be able to restore dignity. People had started to feel ashamed in front of their children for not being able to feed them.

The second wave hit us nine months later, and this time there were no oxygen cylinders and no ventilator beds in India. People world over saw images from India in which people died in parking lots of hospitals, in the backs of trucks and in open fields. We were in the midst of this too. Trying to get people some relief.

Our efforts were small. We were all volunteers. In the many groups that I was part of across the country, most people were also theatre-makers. I found it extraordinary, and I felt extremely proud at the effort theatre-makers were putting in in order to serve people. There are four vital synergies between being a theatre practitioner and relief-worker in India.

First, we need to work in small teams that multi-task. Second, we need to work with very limited resources. Third, we need to reach out to people who are from different walks of life. And finally, we need to raise funds. These are all part of our day-to-day lives.

In India, which is where I have been through this pandemic, theatre-makers across political belief systems jumped in to relief-work almost automatically. Some people organized food relief for millions of migrant workers who had to walk across the country to get back to their villages in the first lockdown. Some provided healthcare support. People went out to bury or burn those whose dead bodies could not be given to their families due to Covid regulations. I have never felt prouder for being a theatre-maker as I did in this time.

I also think so many theatre people were involved in this relief-work in India because they understood the importance of dignity. Being able to provide food or oxygen cylinders in many ways boils down to simple privilege in society. In India, where a person can run out of oxygen by a margin of a hundred dollars, it is not a huge deal to be able to find some means of support through our middle-class means. This is true of most developing nations. There is a new middle class that is about two decades old. In these two decades, we are also the first generation to see such a large gap between the poor and the middle class. Earlier, when we were growing up, we only had the super-rich, the people in the villages and the rest of us. The fact that my generation grew up standing in queues for rice and oil in ration shops perhaps helped us understand what it feels like to not have the opportunity to stand in that queue and get subsidized food essentials. I am not sure our children will know this. They will perhaps do a lot of philanthropy. But we were not doing philanthropy. We were trying to save some other children some of the hardship that many of us had gone through in our lives. The disappointment at standing in ration queues and coming home empty-handed. Most people in my generation have faced that as children to some degree or other.

While this was happening in my life, online there was seminar after seminar about how to save the theatre. Although I do not deny the importance of those seminars, I cannot even begin to explain how meaningless I found them at that time. Not because I think the theatre should not be our concern but because I did not understand how so many people not only took to moving theatre online but also started eulogizing it as the saviour.

How many people in India have an internet connection? How many people can access a smartphone or a laptop in South Asia at large, in Africa, in Iran, in Indonesia, in Philippines or Brazil? What is the connectivity in Harlem like? In East London, in Ipswich and in the favelas of Barcelona? Who can watch a play online in a house with three children, two grandparents and a working couple in the Turkish suburbs of Paris?

I am not sure how the theatre fraternity in urban India, and also significantly in the West, appeared online one day and declared that the online version of theatre was the next big turn in performing arts. I could understand its importance, but for the life of me, I could not understand how could it be deemed as the future of the theatre!

I was on several conversations and interviews in the first few months myself. However, I was clear that these had to be about a subject that deals with the theatre. They could not be about 'How to save the theatre?' A question I am deeply allergic to because I think first and foremost it's the wrong question. It is the question 'How do we save the theatre-maker?' in disguise.

I always attend talks only if they have a specific subject and not something that is a conversation-starter. I do not chat at work. So, I detest these kinds of talks completely.

In contrast, initiatives that did not claim to save the theatre did remarkably well in their humble manner.

An enormous amount of content was made available by leading theatres around the world that made it possible for people like us to see the performances. Although the content was online and not live, I still learnt a lot by watching these performances. My work was performed in many places online and I ended up writing a trilogy during this time: *Raashan* (originally in Hindi), *Salt* and *The Najma Trilogy*. This entire trilogy (including *The Najma Trilogy*) is based on stories of people I encountered in this year of the pandemic. They are daily-wage labour, sex workers, healthcare professionals from poor backgrounds and vagrant alcoholics who drink cheap alcohol to kill hunger. People who are just below the surface of our society. Whose dignities have been compromised enormously due to this pandemic.

This has been one of the busiest years of my life. Our university moved to online classes. Projects started and shut as cities around the world opened and shut one wave after another. I wrote essays in this book and directed a concert theatre piece with two extraordinary musician-actresses on feminism and Shakespeare. While all this was going on, my wife and I were also dealing with our responsibilities at home, our daughter's education, her well-being, the stress with relatives and family elsewhere contracting the virus, the stress of living under severe constraint and its challenges due to multiple lockdowns. However, through all this, the one thing I kept thanking my stars for was that we never had to compromise on our dignity. This is real privilege.

Outside, however, it was mayhem. At one point of time earlier this year, I had about 130 critical cases running at one time, all of whom needed oxygen within six hours. Every day I would lose five to six people. Some patients and some volunteers. It was devastating internally. But externally we kept going. All of us.

Even now, as the second wave has settled, I realize that there have been no borders this year as well. I have had play openings, online and offline, in India, Dubai, Christchurch, New York (on audio), Gothenburg (Sweden) and London.

However, this leads me to ask, what are the borders that we keep talking about. Who is it that separates us from whom?

All the plays I have mentioned are essentially available now to see online. They also played in person in most cases in theatre buildings that do not necessarily reach out to the poor and needy of those cities. Our diversity in theatre is a long way off even now worldwide from the commitment that we claim to have to it. No wonder the theatre fraternity called the online theatre the next best thing, although in reality no one who really needed the healing most urgently, or the questioning of the system, could access these plays.

Which got me thinking about what is the fundamental change that lies ahead of us now.

In our past, subconsciously we were making work for people who would also automatically have a laptop and an internet connection. Since our normal was based on the idea of inequality, the invisible hand and singular identity, we had already removed all these people who were dying without dignity from our theatre thinking. Our ideological fatigue from the last century had led us to a silent chamber of ideology in which we did not realize that ideology is not something we do, it is something we recognize. It exists, whether we like it or not.

No wonder the move to the internet felt so natural to so many people. All the debates ranged around form. Very rarely did it veer to who is this theatre reaching. If our work can reach someone in Christchurch and someone in Ottawa at the click of a button, is there anymore a border? However, if it can never reach the person who lives in the slum three minutes from my house and if the theatre enthusiast in Harlem or East Ham can never see it in their tiny house, what are the new borders? Which are these borders to cross?

IV

The road ahead: The new normal

What lies ahead of us is a life with virus. That is as far as I can see.

Vaccines have arrived in many places in the developed countries. I hear Broadway is about to open. Europe has started to issue the green pass to people from certain countries and with particular vaccines. Through all this we are entering into an era of 'medicitizenship'. Medicitizenship is the phenomenon where a person's fundamental citizenship lies with a set of medical access that the person can have. In the history of evolution, access to food and water, habitation, the right climate to grow have decided which species will survive and which won't. The spread of human species around the world shows us that particular kinds of *Homo sapiens* migrated to particular places for fundamental reasons to do with being able to maintain the body.

In the Anthropocene, this question of survival is closely linked to our medical access. People who have access to vaccination, ventilators, oxygen, cutting-edge research on new mutations and new medicines are invariably going to be part of a different league of citizenship than others. This access is partly going to be the wealth of the country the people are living in, but I think we have enough evidence to see that death and disease penetrate through inequalities in all countries quite rapidly. The so-called First World was ravaged by the first wave of the pandemic. Rome and New York echoed the sounds of sirens night and day.

Hence, I believe we have to understand that the new medicitizen is the person who will have access to the existing infrastructure of theatres. The person who is not part of this elite citizenship will not be able to enter the theatre. It is as simple as that.

However, we as theatre-makers have to ask ourselves if we forever want to make theatre for the medicitizen alone. Will we create theatre in forms that allow the theatre to be mobile? For it to go to places? Will the theatre necessarily need to become mobile and small? Would it not be shameful if as the crisis of the world expands, the theatre shrinks?

Do we need to uphold our buildings inside those buildings? Can they be buildings that focus more on moving their work to places which do not have medicitizens as opposed to catering only to the elite?

This new category also forces us to think of an essential question. An ideological question.

What is the ideology we are in now? Which is to say that if we believe in equality, justice and the greater common good, what are we willing to give up for it?

Ideology is always determined by the cost of ideology. If we seat a communist and a capitalist in the same room, chances are high that both of them will root for health care, education, access to food and water. However, the difference lies in the fact that the communist will seek to give up some freedoms till society is equal while the capitalist will give up some nets of security till society can propel itself to inclusive growth. The difference is not in desire but in method.

However, the question is that if we live in a largely capitalist world and it is glaringly clear that we can no longer throw open our lives to the market, what ideological anchors can we hold on to?

I believe we in the theatre have to lead this conversation. We have to recover from our insecurity about whether we will survive and do our job of asking the big questions. We need to take the modes of healing to those who cannot enter our buildings.

We need to question more actively our inequities, power structures and beliefs with the ones who can enter the building.

We have to give birth to the next ideological frameworks through our plays and performances.

We, the theatre-makers, have to give ourselves the ambition to unfurl and unpack the question of what are we willing to give up in order to stand up for our beliefs.

We need to stop asking the question 'How will the theatre change after the pandemic?' and ask instead the golden question unapologetically, 'How will the theatre change the world?'

It is time to stop being a mirror.

BIBLIOGRAPHY

Al-Biruni, Abu Rayhan (2015), *Alberuni's India*, trans. Edward Sachau, New Delhi: Rupa Publications.
Ali, Agha Shahid (1998), *The Country Without a Post Office: Poems*, New York: W. W. Norton & Company.
Aristotle (1996), *Poetics*, London: Penguin Classics.
Beckett, Samuel (2010), *Waiting for Godot*, London: Faber.
Bharata Muni (1950), *Natya Shastra*, Newark: Facsimile Publisher.
Bogart, Anne (2001), *A Director Prepares: Seven Essays on Art and Theatre*, Abingdon: Routledge.
Brecht, Bertolt (1999), *The Caucasian Chalk Circle*, trans. Eric Bentley, Minneapolis: University of Minnesota Press.
Brecht, Bertolt (2017), *War Primer*, ed. John Willett, New York: Verso Books.
Chakrabarti, Lolita (2020), *Red Velvet*, North Yorkshire: Methuen Drama.
Euripides (2001), *The Trojan Women and Other Plays*, trans. James Morwood, Oxford: Oxford University Press.
Ferdowsi, Abolqasem (2016), *Shahnameh: The Persian Book of Kings*, trans. Dick Davis, London: Penguin Classics.
Fugard, Athol (1994), *Playland*, New York: Samuel French.
Fugard, Athol (2009), *"Master Harold" . . . and the Boys: A Play*, New York: Vintage.
Goodman, Paul (1972), *Speaking and Language: Defence of Poetry*, New York: Vintage.
Grass, Günter (1966), *The Plebeians Rehearse the Uprising: A German Tragedy*, Boston: Mariner Books.
Hansberry, Lorraine (2002), *A Raisin in the Sun*, New York: Random House.
Hansberry, Lorraine (2009), *Les Blancs*, New York: Samuel French.
Heruka, Tsangnyön (2010), *The Life of Milarepa*, trans. Andrew Quintman, London: Penguin Classics.
Homer (1999), *The Iliad*, trans. Robert Fagles, London: Penguin Classics.
Homer (2006), *The Odyssey*, trans. Robert Fagles, London: Penguin Classics.

Khoudry, Elias (2016), *Gate of the Sun*, trans. Humphrey Davies, New York: Archipelago Books.
Kushner, Tony (2017), *Angels in America: Millennium Approaches & Perestroika*, London: Nick Hern Books.
Mishra, Pankaj (2013), *From the Ruins of Empire: The Revolt Against the West and the Remaking of Asia*, London: Picador.
Morton, Timothy (2013), *Hyperobjects: Philosophy and Ecology after the End of the World*, Minneapolis: University of Minnesota Press.
Naipaul, Vidiadhar Surajprasad (1990), *A Turn in the South*, New York: Vintage.
Piketty, Thomas (2020), *Capital and Ideology*, trans. Arthur Goldhammer, Cambridge: Belknap Press.
Roy, Arundhati (1998), *The God of Small Things*, New York: Harper Collins.
Shakespeare, William (2005), *The Oxford Shakespeare. The Complete Works*, Oxford: Oxford University Press.
Shōgo, Ōta (1990), 'The Water Station (Mizu no Eki)', trans. Mari Boyd, *Asian Theatre Journal*, 7 (2).
Smith, Adam (1977), *An Inquiry into the Nature and Causes of the Wealth of Nations*, Chicago: University of Chicago Press.
Sophocles (1984), *The Three Theban Plays: Antigone, Oedipus the King, Oedipus at Colonus*, trans. Robert Fagles, London: Penguin Classics.
Soyinka, Wole (1965), *The Road*, Oxford: Oxford University Press.
Soyinka, Wole (2002), *Death and the King's Horseman: A Play*, New York: W. W. Norton & Company.
The Arabian Nights: Tales from a Thousand and One Nights (2004), trans. Richard Burton, New York: Modern Library Classics.
The Epic of Gilgamesh (2002), trans. Andrew George, London: Penguin Classics.
Thiong'o, Ngugi wa (2011), *Decolonising the Mind: The Politics of Language in African Literature*, Melton, Suffolk: James Currey Ltd.
Valmiki (1976), *Ramayana*, trans. William Buck, Oakland: University of California Press.
Vogel, Paula (2018), *How I Learned to Drive*, New York: Theatre Communications Group.
Vyasa (2009), *The Mahabharata*, trans. John D. Smith, London: Penguin Classics.
Wakhlu, Somnath N. (1994), *Habba Khatoon: The Nightingale of Kashmir*, New Delhi: Roli Books.
Wilson, August (2015), *The Piano Lesson*, New York: Samuel French.
Wolfe, George C. (1988), *The Colored Museum*, New York: Grove Press.